CHARLES BRONSON
THE KRAYS AND ME

CHARLES BRONSON
THE KRAYS AND ME

CHARLIE BRONSON
With Stephen Richards

JOHN BLAKE

Published by John Blake Publishing Ltd,
3 Bramber Court, 2 Bramber Road,
London W14 9PB, England

www.blake.co.uk

First published in paperback in 2007

ISBN: 978 1 84454 325 0

British Library Cataloguing-in-Publication Data:

A catalogue record for this book is available from the British Library.

Design by www.envydesign.co.uk

Printed in the UK by CPI Bookmarque, Croydon, CR0 4TD

5 7 9 10 8 6

Papers used by John Blake Publishing are natural, recyclable products made
from wood grown in sustainable forests. The manufacturing processes
conform to the environmental regulations of the country of origin.

For Charlie, Ronnie and Reggie
Brothers in arms

FOREWORD

Life with the Krays was brilliant. In fact, despite the long years I've now spent in prison, my whole life has been brilliant – I've no regrets, I loved it all! Hell, I've even married whilst behind bars. I've hope, faith and a future.

I was and still am in total solitary. I'm still labelled Britain's number one madman. I recall when I was taken to the courts of appeal in the Strand for a brief legal argument appearance. Ten guards, armoured van! Security! It probably cost the taxpayers ten grand to take me there! I got there and the three appeal court judges say, 'You are too dangerous to be allowed into the court room.' So my application for leave to appeal went on without me. I was locked in the dungeon cell below the court; while my life was being discussed, I wasn't allowed to hear it. Well, why the fuck take me there in the first place, what's the point? Ten grand wasted. I know the Krays felt the same as me about their time inside: prison is a joke – a farce! When my appeal proper took place on 1 April, I was allowed access to the court ... but so what! I lost the appeal and now face uncertainity over my future. As Justice Rose said, it's all in the hands of the parole board. Yeah, just like it was with Reggie Kray, eh!

CONTENTS

INTRODUCTION

The names of Reggie and Ronnie Kray are synonymous with the 1960s gangland era. Their notorious gang's reign of terror over the lower echelons of London's criminal community ceased in 1969, when the Kray twins and their henchmen were remanded to Brixton Prison for murder.

At the time, I was just seventeen years old and on remand up in Risley Jail, in Warrington, for nicking a furniture lorry – slightly different to what the Krays faced.

Had I been around in the Kray days, then there is no doubt that I would have become embroiled in their activities ... but I wasn't, and neither were half of the others who supposedly had a connection to what became known as 'the Firm'. Everyone from the candlestick maker to the undertaker, it seems, has a story to tell about the Krays. Glorified fucking autograph hunters!

I remember that a lot of the lads in the prison had the twins' photos out of the newspaper up on their cell walls, as if supporting them for some cause – yeah, 'Vote for the Krays' sort of thing! I suppose that was the first time I really took an interest in them; let's face it, they were the 'crème de la crème' of the criminal fraternity. All us young prisoners (Y/Ps) looked up to people like them. These were 'real' gangsters, not cardboard cut-outs.

During the course of the next 29 years, I was to become a close and trusted confidant of the Kray twins ... closer than any of their so-called self-proclaimed henchmen!

Everything I've read about Ronnie and Reggie Kray since their death is a load of BOLLOCKS! Just recently, one story said they probably killed thirty. 'Probably!' 'Maybe!' 'Could have!' 'I bet they did!!' In ten years' time, the tally will be three hundred!

Then there are the maggots crawling out to sell a story:

'Ronnie beat my dad up and gave him seven hundred stitches!'

'Reggie ran over my hamster!'

'I'm Ronnie's daughter!'

'Reggie shot my cat!'

'I'm Reggie's son!'

It's just laughable! Why didn't these people say these things when the Krays were alive? Gutless rats and maggots spreading rumours with their sham stories for sale.

Well, since the twins have passed away, I can now talk about a few things myself. This is my tribute to them: No Bollocks – No Silly Stories – Just Facts! Facts about the time I spent doing porridge with the Krays; about how they survived inside. And, let me tell you, I've got a lot to say and all the time in the world to say it.

The truth is, they were gentlemen. Great guys. Dangerous if you crossed them, but only a fool would do that – then again, the planet is full of fools! There's never been a book on the Krays quite like this one – though, no doubt, many will follow it!

This book will amaze you all. Parts of it will shock you, but, believe me now, forget all the shit you've read about them up to now – all those people claiming they were great pals with the Krays – 'cos most of it isn't fact.

What follows is a short recap on each of the Kray brothers. I don't want to spiel on too much about what you probably already know, so I will try to keep it as short as possible.

CHARLIE KRAY 1927–2000 (RIP)

I met Charlie in Parkhurst many years ago when he used to visit his twin brothers. Later, I would see him in Broadmoor when he used to visit Ronnie. Charlie always left some meat pies for me with the Broadmoor nurses, just like his mum Violet used to do. I'd look forward to scoffing them, and I've never forgotten his act.

Charlie's most certainly a legend and he was a very proud man, a well-respected man. He served ten years for nothing, just because he was the brother of the Kray twins.

He got out and picked up the pieces, but it all went pear shaped for him later on and things turned to mush when he was convicted of drug dealing – all for a few grand up in Newcastle! Everyone knew it was a stitch-up, 'cos the deal Charlie was accused of putting together was so impossible! He was to have supplied a few million pounds' worth of drugs over a period of time. The real story is, he was just using the Kray name to make a few quid out of a possible deal in which he'd be a middle man. Anyone in the underworld will tell you that the thing wasn't likely to happen, but the law in its infinite wisdom decided to believe a load of plonkers. Charlie was never to live down the shame of being connected with drugs, something the Kray twins never really delved into.

Sadly, it came at a bad time for Charlie and, when he was banged up in Durham Prison in 1999, he soon came down with an illness and was moved to Parkhurst, which had been demoted from a category 'A' prison to a category 'B' prison – the regime was more relaxed for him there than at Durham. When Charlie declined still further in health, he had to be moved to St Mary's Hospital on the Isle of Wight.

He passed away in the hospital in 2000 and, once again, Reg had to attend the funeral of another member of his family. Charlie was and always will be Ron and Reg's big brother – God bless you, mate.

We all loved Charlie – he was from the old school and my respects for him come from my family along with me.

REGGIE KRAY 1933–2000 (RIP)

They sent Reg to Parkhurst SSU (Special Segregation Unit) in the 1960s, where the Richardsons were – they were rivals! Clearly, the authorities had hoped that the two sets of gangsters would kill each other – that's how evil the prison HQ is: they want blood. But it was obvious to the Krays and the Richardsons what was going on, and they agreed that their inhumane sentences were enough to handle without adding on more trouble.

I last saw Reg in Gartree Prison in the Eighties. It was through him that I became involved in the unlicensed fight game. Reg helped set up my first fight on the Paul Edmunds (RIP) show, as later seen on my video documentary, Sincerely Yours.

I've got some good memories of Reg. I remember the time he knocked out O'Rooke in Parkhurst with one punch (I later stuck a sauce bottle in O'Rooke's face). Reg had a heart as big as the sky and it's a fact that he helped many a con out of trouble. He took weapons off young cons and gave them good advice, he sat down with cons that had given up, and he even prayed for some. He had become a born-again Christian.

A lot of bad press has been thrown in Reg's direction over the years. A few years ago, it was stated that he was taking drugs; well, that's a load of rubbish. He trained every day, and at 64 he had the body of a thirty-year-old – a man on drugs couldn't possibly have been in such good shape. Reg watched his diet, he was a fitness fanatic, he despised drugs and I know it saddened him to have to read such lies. The propaganda machine of the Home Office was busy working away putting out their lies while Reg rotted away – both in prison and inside himself.

Reg had married Frances Shea on 20 April 1965; they lived in a flat below Ron. Frances was the love of Reg's life. Later, when Frances committed suicide at the age of 23 – she took an overdose – it really knocked the wind out of Reg's sails. It was said that he was never the same man ever again. Reg later told me that he was quite depressed by the time Nipper Read of Scotland Yard arrested him.

Although a number of fringe members tried to hold the gang together, it seemed Reg had accepted the inevitable. Had some of the gang members put their hands up to the murder charges then Reg would have been in the clear over the McVitie killing, and he would have submitted a guilty plea to the lesser charges. This, though, did not happen. The Kray gang collapsed under pressure from failings within when some of the gang turned Queen's Evidence … thus Reg was found guilty and given thirty years' imprisonment. That tariff was more than met, but it would seem that the judiciary had failed to carry out what one of their representatives had stated more than thirty years previously. By the time Reg died, he had served nearly 32 years. Thirty-two years of shit to get where he is today – in a box in the ground! He'd done no wrong to any man who didn't deserve it, and he was a well-respected man.

He helped this one and that one, supported charities in prison as he had done when he was free, helped little old ladies, supported boxing clubs, and generally used his influence to protect those who were weak and unable to defend themselves. He followed all the rules laid down and yet he was treated worse than some greasy evil paedophile. Was that right?

I bet if they asked the public whether they'd rather have some stinking child killer like Ian Huntley or someone like Reg living next door to them, Reg would win the vote hands down every single time. But what does it matter now that he's dead.

When Reg was alive, I made it clear that I thought the whole question of his continued imprisonment stank. Reg had a campaign going for his release but, because it had been going on for years, it become a bit of a regular thing like the annual ball and that was the problem – there was too much of a laid-back approach by his supporters. Reg made it clear that all he wanted was to have a little cottage to end his days in, but it wasn't to be.

RONNIE KRAY 1933–1995, 'THE COLONEL' (RIP)

On 17 March 1995, I woke up as I did every other day. I ate my porridge and went out in the exercise cage for my hour of exercise. The air was fresh and the sky was lovely; even the sun was shining, which is a rare thing up in the frozen north – I was in the most northerly of

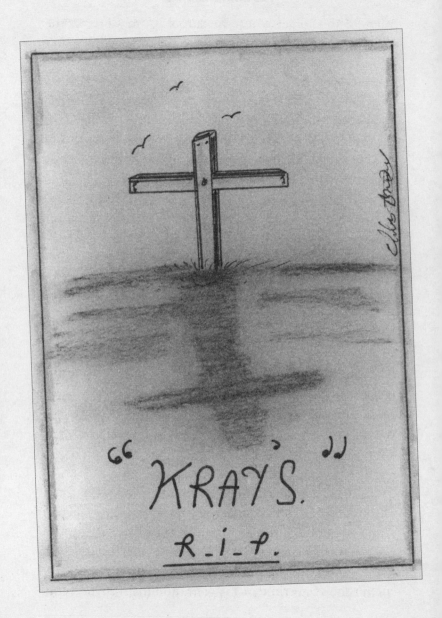

England's max-secure prisons, Frankland Prison's maximum secure block.

I'll never forget the news that hit me like a sledgehammer on the back of the head that day. While out on the yard, I lost one of the greatest friends I ever had – Ronnie Kray passed away.

I'm now gonna put the record straight once and for all. During the first few days of his death I heard maggots going on about how mad and bad Ronnie was. The press and radio ripped him up, but what did they know? Ronnie Kray was a special man and he had the biggest heart of any criminal I've ever known. There won't ever be another like him. I'm gonna tell you something now: Ronnie Kray was a legend, he was born a legend, lived a legend and died a legend.

Reggie kept the flag flying for Ron, and Ron wanted so desperately for Reg to go free. And he looked after me too – just a week before Ron's death, he sent me some money; he loved me.

When Ron liked somebody, it was total loyalty; he was a man of great feelings and great warmth. I can close my eyes and drift back three decades ago to when Ron walked into my cell at Parkhurst. I knew from our first ever meet that he was a special friend – a handshake like a grip of steel and eyes that were full of strength. He conducted himself inside no differently to the way he did outside – with dignity.

When Ron spoke, people listened, I learned so much from him. He was always polite and respectful and never spoke of crime or violence, and he lived by a code of honour till the end. Sure, Ron was violent, we all know that, but many only knew that side of him, they didn't get to know the other side.

I was certified insane a year before Ron, and we met up again in Broadmoor. We both suffered from mental problems, and I feel that brought us closer in a way. Parkhurst made Ronnie very ill; violence breeds violence and Parkhurst is a place of violence. Ronnie was a target there, but, once in Broadmoor, he quickly settled.

In the fifteen years he was there, he had very little in the way of problems, which only proves what I say. Parkhurst made him ill, but Ronnie took to Broadmoor like an Eskimo takes to ice. If you're insane, it's a permanent state, but drugs helped keep Ron stable.

Do you know what Ronnie did for most of his 26 years while caged up? I'll tell you: he helped people. He'd read something in a newspaper – let's say a little kid had an illness or an old lady got mugged – and straight away he would set about trying to raise money to help that person in trouble. He'd paint a picture, write a poem or organise a charity do, all to help the sick. He literally gave away thousands of pounds, if not a million, in good causes.

All his life, Ronnie Kray gave. He actually cried over tragedies, especially when kids were involved. He despised child abusers. God help it if he were still alive today ... Ian Huntley wouldn't have lasted five minutes if he had been sectioned off to Broadmoor. Ron was always first to go and help the underdog. He never did it to boost his ego or to be the big shot, he did it for one simple reason, and that was he couldn't help it, he was ruled by his feelings. Ronnie looked after so many, he never stopped helping – it's why he's so special, so loved and will never be forgotten by so many.

Ron and Reg had a dear friend, Steph, who was close to them. She wrote to me after his death to say that Ron wouldn't want me to be upset and that he had loved me a lot. Ron always got upset when he heard about my constant battles against the system. He used to write to me – when I'd been up on a roof or taken a hostage – telling me to slow down or I'd never get out. He cared about me and understood me and I read his words like they were from my own father. Steph wrote: 'Ron's free and he's now with the only woman he ever loved.' That about sums up Ron Kray, Steph's written it in once sentence and she's so right. 'He's with his beloved mother, Violet, the only woman he adored.'

Ron was born on 17 October 1933, in Hoxton, East London, the second of the twins. Violet said of the twins when they were born that they were 'so lovely, like two little black-haired dolls'. Although Ronnie was always polite, this exterior image belied the power he held over Reg. Ronnie was always there to see to it that Reg won his battles and, afterwards, Reg would find it hard to face Ron if he came off second best. Reg summed it up when he said: 'He (Ron) would be a sort of conscience and I found it hard to face him afterwards.' Ron was born ten minutes after Reg but it seemed he wanted to lead the way.

Years later, this could have had some bearing in the Jack 'the Hat' McVitie murder. Reg pulled the trigger of his Beretta, which he was holding to McVitie's head, and it didn't go off! Different stories abound as to what happened next. Some say Ron, who came in with four male dancers in tow, handed Reg a knife and told him to 'do him'. Obviously, with a room full of people standing about, it wasn't gonna be easy for Reg to back down and lose face – he had to go through with it, 'cos otherwise he'd find it hard to face Ron afterwards.

Ron told me what really happened that night. Tony Lambrianou brought McVitie to the party, McVitie was told to sit down, the gun was placed to his head ... click, click, nothing happened. Then, McVitie shouted, 'You let Dixon go!' (A reference to the fact that Ron had pulled the trigger of a gun that failed to go off when he had intended to kill George Dixon – Dixon was let off with a warning.) Ron replied, 'Yeah, but we ain't letting you off! You've taken too many liberties.'

A struggle took place. McVitie was no weakling, he broke free from Reg and ran while Ron was bad-mouthing him. After McVitie was dragged back through a window he had part smashed by trying to dive out of it, Ron said, 'Be a man, Jack.' McVitie replied, 'Yeah, but I won't fucking die like one.'

Reg was handed a carving knife ... the rest is history. Reg admitted to me that he had nightmares about the killing afterwards.

* * * * *

Going right back to the beginning, the first court appearance of the twins was at the Old Bailey back in 1950, after a sixteen-year-old lad was beaten up with fists, boots and chains; the case was thrown out for lack of evidence .

Reg and Ronnie both turned pro-boxers in 1951 and started out as lightweights, though Ron wasn't as skilled as Reg in the noble art of pugilistic skills.

Their first HQ was a billiard hall and from there they started up 'the Firm'. Ronnie got his nickname 'The Colonel' after being dismissed from the army. Although Reggie was an effective fighter and organiser, Ronnie seemed to become increasingly adept at taking the initiative when necessary. After one prolonged briefing with a group of their followers, one of them said, 'Christ, Ron, you're just like a bloody colonel.'

Their reign spread over all of London but that didn't prevent them having run-ins with other up-and-coming firms, the most notorious of which was the aforementioned Richardson gang.

Ronnie loved to dress like a gangster, and he even had his own barber to help him keep up appearances, but, even though he was tough, maybe we see a little bit of the fear we've all got within us when I tell you that he used to sleep with the light on. He was just as vulnerable as the next man when it came to trying to conquer his inner fears – we've all got our own battles going on inside our heads; Ron was no different.

On one occasion, a docker who claimed Ronnie had shot him later went on to pick him out of an ID parade.

Ron went on the ID parade and must have thought he'd ended the matter after he told them, 'I'm not Ronnie Kray, I'm Reg. I wasn't nowhere near when this bloke was shot.'

The case was dropped, but Reg wasn't too happy with Ronnie, saying, 'You must be raving mad, you shoot a man and leave me to clear it up.' Ronnie spat back, 'All you're fit for is clearing up, you couldn't shoot a man if you tried!' Maybe this was what motivated Reg to pull the gun on Jack McVitie so as to show Ronnie he was able to shoot a man after all, but if the truth was known Reg would've walked away from it until Ron came in. From that point on, Reg was caught in a trap – no way out.

This rivalry seems to have followed through to the end of their days on the streets of London. Reg was put in a position of not only having to keep face with the crowd at the private party where McVitie was stabbed to death, but also having to keep face with Ronnie. Reg was committed to killing McVitie just by duress of circumstance, which is a plea in itself. Had Reg been able to show the court that, indeed, he might have faced the wrath of his brother, Ron, had he not gone through with the killing, then this could have been mitigation and he might have been walking the streets years ago, but pride comes before a fall. Reg was as loyal to Ron as Ron was to Reg. Brother going against brother didn't come into the equation. After the death of his brothers, Ronnie and Charlie, he had to carry the flag of honour on his own shoulders.

Should Reg have been found guilty of involvement in the attack against Martin then this would have added credible evidence against him to support what people believe, which was that Reg had a violent streak equal to his brother, Ron. Why, though, was it that Ron seemed to amass a record of violence over and above Reg's record? When Ron was out of the way, behind bars, Reg always kept his nose to the grinding wheel of business, even lambasting Ron for ruining everything he had built up. As much as Reg was the builder of their empire, then, surely, Ron was the destructive force behind the Kray empire.

The set of circumstances around the killing of McVitie shows that Reg had no way out, no escape route so as he could back down from what Ron wanted him to do, not without losing face. And that was a big no no!

The most famous club owned by Ron and Reg was called The Double R, and it was in Bow Road, London. The Double R was doing well in the late 1950s and was heavily populated by celebrities. Ron, though, was still in prison. He was becoming increasingly prone to bouts of depression, which led to him being declared insane at the age of 24.

Ron was sent to an asylum in February 1958 but soon made a recovery. During one Sunday visit, Reg swapped places with Ron, who was eventually sent back to prison after his family tried and failed to help him with his problems. Ron was drugged up and handed over to the authorities by his own despairing family. What else could they do?

When Ron was released, he came out a changed man. He now looked quite different to Reg. The time behind bars had taken its toll on him. Something had changed – maybe being apart from his other half was to blame, but whatever the reason it looked like Ron would have to carry the scars of mental torment. He soon became difficult to control and Reg, it was rumoured, wasn't too pleased about the situation. Reg had to go away to serve time and when Ron took over the reins of The Double R club it seemed to go downhill.

Ronnie wasn't ashamed of his sexuality – which didn't make him too fashionable in London at the time – but he always kept his dignity by maintaining he wasn't a 'poof' but that he was 'homosexual'. At least he was man enough to accept what he was, and long before we had Quentin Crisp parading his weak-kneed act in TV's The Naked Civil Servant. No limp-wristedness was on show here and, at least, Ronnie set new standards for others to follow.

Everybody knows the story of the fatal incident in the Blind Beggar pub in 1966, when Ron shot a guy called George Cornell 'cos he supposedly called him 'a fat poof'. That wasn't the case at all. According to Frankie Fraser, this was just hype. In reality, Cornell was rumoured to have been present when a cousin of the twins, Richard Hart, was shot dead in a nightclub at 3.30am on 8 March 1966. Indeed, it was suggested that Cornell pulled the trigger of the gun that killed Hart. A swift response by Ronnie resulted in the untimely death of Cornell. Of course, after the shooting, nobody could remember what went on or who did it – bad memories were a good thing to have back then. Lots of people went missing – lots – but only those who deserved to go went. If you believe the press, it would seem that the Krays were responsible for every crime in London at the time but, in reality, they did more good than bad.

I met Ronnie in Parkhurst and later on in Broadmoor and, as usual, he was the perfect gentleman. He stopped me from sorting a few eggheads out. His most famous saying to me was: 'Madness is a gift of life, it's how you use it that counts.'

CHAPTER 1

THE BEGINNING
OF THE END

Let me tell you a fact, if you read all the Krays' books, you'll notice most of them have different stories about the same event. Take Frank Mitchell's murder and the claims made as to how his body was disposed of. Some say that he was chopped into pieces and fed into a meat mincer. Others, that if he ain't inside a motorway bridge or fed to pigs, then he was wrapped up in wire and fed to the fish. One book even says he's living in South America. Each of the Kray books is now becoming more and more hard to believe.

So, you may ask, then why have I written one? Good question! Simple – my story on the Krays is from the inside. I personally don't give a fuck if Mitchell's in a tin of cat food!

The Frank Mitchell story goes on and on, and now Mitchell has become a legend! Although Dartmoor was a place where inmates were routinely abused and degraded by prison officers, this wasn't the case with our Frank – he did the abusing! In jail, Frank was a feared figure and he would easily get his own way with prison staff – although he was once flogged for beating a prison officer senseless.

In 1955 he was declared mentally defective and sent to Rampton. After escaping from Rampton in 1957, he broke into a house and used an iron bar to attack the owner.

During the police operation to capture Frank, he used a pair of meat cleavers to resist arrest; this led to him being sent to Broadmoor. Soon after this, he escaped, broke into another house and was said to have attacked the occupants with an axe. In reality he did little more than break into an old couple's house and hold them captive with an axe he found in their garden shed. He did nothing more than force them to watch television with him while he drank tea with the axe neatly balanced across his knees. This led to a life sentence being imposed on him and the newspapers labelling him the 'Mad Axeman'. Although Frank was a fanatical bodybuilder and weightlifter, his brainpower did not match his size or strength. He could be lured into anything if the reward fitted what he desired. Although Frank was described as a violent and brutal psychopath, in reality he was as far removed from that description as he could possibly be. Anecdotal evidence points to Frank being nothing more than a gentle giant.

For some reason, Frank was subsequently deemed mentally stable and was sent to Dartmoor, where his behaviour took a turn for the better. Whilst at Dartmoor, Frank started breeding budgerigars, which could have resulted in him becoming known as the 'Birdman of Dartmoor', though it wouldn't have sounded as good as the 'Mad Axeman'!

By September 1966, the marked improvement in Frank's behaviour led to him being allowed to work on the outside of the prison in what was called an 'Honour Party'.

During the course of working outside of the prison, Frank would take advantage of the low security applied to him and traipse off to local pubs, always returning back to prison for the end of work. As long as he was back in time for the evening roll call he was left to his own devices.

The Home Office had not issued Frank with a release date from his life sentence and he became disgruntled. Word of this soon reached the Kray gang in London.

In an undated letter to the Krays, released by the Public Record Office, Mitchell complained about the alleged conspiracy to send him back to Broadmoor. He wrote: 'Anyway, my dears, I can always crash out of there again. I know once I get there I ain't going to ever get to get out the right way.'

On 12 December 1966, Frank was picked up from Dartmoor Prison by members of the notorious Kray gang and whisked away to a flat prepared for him in

Barking Road, East Ham, London. The friendship Frank had with Ronnie and Reggie Kray had started years before in Wandsworth Prison. Frank kept up this relationship and often wrote to Ron telling him of his frustration at not being given a review date for his case.

Not surprisingly, the escape made headlines and sparked the biggest manhunt in British criminal history. Exactly why Frank was sprung from the clink is not clear, but such a powerful man could only add to the dimension of the Kray gang. One theory as to why the Kray gang broke Frank free was that it was done purely to highlight the fact that he hadn't been given a release date and that if they could keep him out long enough without him getting into trouble then the Home Office would have to consider his case.

Being cooped up in a small flat led Frank to become agitated, so the Krays brought in Lisa, a blonde nightclub hostess, to keep Frank from becoming bored. Soon after this, Frank told some of the Kray minders that he was going to marry her.

The springing of Frank seemed to have brought problems with it. Within days of Frank escaping, two letters landed at *The Times* and the *Daily Mirror* newspapers asking the Home Secretary for a release date for Frank Mitchell. Frank's thumbprint appeared at the bottom of each letter, to prove that it was actually him who had written them.

This prompted the Home Secretary to appear on

national TV advising Mitchell to hand himself in. Fear started to spread amidst the Kray gang that Mitchell was becoming a liability and that he might talk and give the game away about who had freed him if he was caught! Frank was now starting to make more and more threats, saying that if the twins didn't come to see him then he would go to them. A solution to the problem had to be found!

An allegation was made that a plan was hatched by the Krays to kill Frank. The story goes that he was told by the Kray gang that he was being moved to a place in the country. The next day, 22 or 23 September 1966, a van arrived that was supposed to transport Frank to safety, but, as he stepped out to get in the van, three shots rang out, followed by a further two shots.

During the Old Bailey trial, in 1969, another gangland figure, Albert Donoghue, gave evidence against Freddie Foreman, the Kray twins and their brother, Charlie. But the judge ruled that, because Donoghue was also involved in Mitchell's escape from prison, his evidence could not be accepted without corroboration. Freddie and the Krays were acquitted. In a later admission, Ron Kray said that some Greek men murdered Frank, which is what Ron told me.

The story goes that Frank's new-found love, Lisa, dashed out and confronted Ronnie Kray, shouting, 'They've shot him. Oh, God, they've shot him!' Ronnie Kray, it has been alleged in some other books, later told another gang member, 'He's fucking dead. We had to get rid of him; he would have got us all nicked. We made a mistake getting the bastard out in the first place.'

Three years after the killing of Frank Mitchell in 1966, the Kray twins, Freddie Foreman and several other associates stood accused of murdering Frank: they were found not guilty. At a later trial, Reg Kray received five years' imprisonment for freeing Frank Mitchell from Dartmoor and another nine months for harbouring him, to run concurrently with his other sentences.

Debate has continued as to where the body of Frank Mitchell was disposed of. Possible locations have included the concrete of the Bow Road flyover, the heating boilers of the local baths, the boilers of Southwark Power Station and the sea off Newhaven Harbour. It's also been suggested that he was cremated by one of the Firm who was also a crematorium worker.

Following the escape of Frank Mitchell in 1966, and that of another con called George Blake, developments in the treatment of offenders were inevitably held back. The Prison Department found itself involved in a heavy programme of tightening up security and a report on prison security by Earl Mountbatten.

It was rumoured that, on hearing of Frank Mitchell's death, Reggie cried! Many years later, a Kray gang associate, Freddie Foreman, stated that he had been the gunman, although it is thought by many that another Kray associate played that role. Frank Mitchell – RIP.

* * * * *

It has been claimed that the murder of Jack 'the Hat' McVitie brought on the downfall of the Krays' empire, and also the empires of a lot of other people. Alan Bruce Cooper, an American who was already a registered informer working for a copper called John du Rose (one of Nipper Read's colleagues), was one of the first to make a statement. Cooper would've been charged with offences had he not been a registered informer.

Then there was the statement of a man called Paul Elvey, a bag man who used to run dynamite from Glasgow to London in a briefcase. The dynamite was obtained from coalmines in the Glasgow area hence the connection between Glasgow and London when it comes to hard cases. Elvey was nicked for this but had to be used as a witness when his connection to to Rose was pointed out to Nipper Read of Scotland Yard.

Nipper Read finally had his day on 9 May 1968, when he arrested most of the Kray gang members and charged them all with 'conspiracy to murder persons unknown' – a holding charge. While the gang were locked up it was possible for Read to work away on potential witnesses and he came up trumps with certain people who felt safe enough to come forward with the Krays locked up. Freddie Foreman was also arrested as well as Charlie Kray but, being the true staunch people they were, nothing could be extracted from them. There was more chance of extracting information from a disused coalmine than these two.

A surprise witness was gang member Albert

Donoghue. Donoghue had no reason to feel any loyalty to the gang, as Reg had shot him in the foot in a barroom argument. Ronnie Hart was another gang member who stood in the dock pointing his finger at Ron and Reg. Their fate was sealed.

Charlie Kray was tried and sentenced to ten years as an accomplice to the McVitie murder. He wound up serving seven years of his sentence.

CHAPTER 2

DOING TIME IS EASY

As I mentioned right at the start of this book, when the twins and the Firm were on remand in Brixton, in 1969, I was also on remand up in Risley Jail, in Warrington. Two Scousers and me had nicked this big lorry full of furniture and we were on our way south to flog it all. I pulled into a café at Cannock, on the A5. I had done well to get that far. After all, I had only hit half a dozen cars up to then – I just could not get it right going round corners!

Oh, and I hit a lamppost too. But I still thought that things were going well, until I pulled out of the café. CRASH! That car must have been speeding, as when I pulled out there was no sign of it. Then it was on us! One of the two Scousers let out a scream, and it was under us! My right leg got smashed, my ankle exploded, but my instinct told me to get away!

I knew the café people would be on the scene and the pigs would be there in minutes. Then there'd be an ambulance ...

There was dog shit I could do, so I shouted to the other two, 'Run!' They sat there like lumps of shit! I limped off, dived through a hedge and lay there. I was right, the Old Bill were there in no time!

My leg was in a terrible mess! The pain was agony, but I made a move. It took me a good day to get home. At this time I was living with my mum and dad – and no sooner had I landed home than I was arrested! I told Mum not to worry, and off I went, all cuffed up.

Down at the station, I found the other two. Both made statements: 'It was him.' The usual shit. Both got bail; I got remanded. But I was in big trouble – the driver of the car was on life support. They were waiting to see if he died – if he did, I'd be done with manslaughter! This was a bad spell for me, as it shook me up big time. But I want to say now, that car was speeding. Even the cops said so, having looked at the skids.

If I had had a licence, insurance and had been a lorry driver I'd have been in the clear. But I was a thief and I was in trouble.

Grisly Risley Remand Centre had to be the biggest hellhole on the planet. It had more suicides than any other jail. (Our visits were closed, and only for twenty minutes.) But we had a laugh; on the Y/Ps wing we could stick our heads through the window bars and see the women's wing! You wouldn't believe what these bitches got up to! Legs dangling out the windows! Tits! Bums! And at night … it was brilliant (well, we were only kids). I used to be at my window all night, standing there and looking with a big hard-on! (I told you prison is evil.) It was during this period in my life that I began to perform my acts of strength. Squatting people on my back – three at a time. Then I'd get three or four of the lads to sit on the top bunk, and I'd lift it up! I'd train all day, eat like a horse and basically enjoy myself. That was until the screws started their games!

One of these incidents, I recall, happened after I had just cleaned a floor. It was spotless, and then the fat rat screw kicked my mop bucket over (on purpose), so I picked the bucket up (on purpose) and smashed it in his fat face … accidentally! (Well, accidents do happen …) And then it all started up: beating, choky and punishment. The screw's mates got on my case, which resulted in more violence, more beatings and it went on and on. There was no end. I was down as a lunatic and suffered big time.

Back in those days, in the block, they took your bed off you at 7.30am and you got it back at 7.30pm. All you had in your cell was a piss pot, a water jug and a bible! So you either sat on the floor and felt sorry for yourself, or you fought it! I'd smash on the door all day. Shout at them, abuse them, then I'd do my press-ups and walk up and down. I'd sing a lot too.

By the time 7.30 in the evening came, I was ready for a sleep! Yeah, Risley was a hellhole! Then it comes:

you're on your way to court! The driver of the car that hit the stolen wagon I was driving pulled through! (It was the biggest relief ever.) The charges I was left with amounted to taking and driving away. Underage, no licence, no insurance, dangerous driving and all the usual crap ... I was expecting Borstal! But, to my surprise, I escaped with probation – plus a big fine, plus a life ban. I actually got a right result. But I'll say now, I'm sorry for that crash. It was a total accident – but if that driver hadn't been speeding then it would never have happened.

Then I was free again. It was down Tommy Powell's club, where my aunty Eileen worked as waitress. I used to pop in there and see if she was OK. Who should walk in but one of the rats who had been in the lorry. We soon got it on – it ended up outside in the street. I enjoyed punching his face in!

Pity the twins never had any luck. It's crazy how life is – what if that driver had died? If, if, if ... ah, why bother!

I met Harry Jacobs ('Mad H') in 1974, in the long-term wing workshop of Walton Jail. He had just left Parkhurst C Unit and come up to Walton for accumulated visits. Mad H really was the original psycho. I'd rate him amongst the top ten most dangerous – he oozed violence, it was all over his face ... but I got on great with him!

Now, remember, I had just got my sentence at this time; Harry had done years. One day, he was chatting and he was going on about the twins, blah, blah, blah.

Some Scouser said, 'I bet he never even met them.' Harry went white and began to shake, and I could see it about to go off!

'Yeah,' the Scouser said, 'I bet it's all shit. I bet you've never even had the birch!'

Harry had been telling us about the birch days before. He stood up and ripped off his shirt: his back was a mass of welts. That said it all. But I'll say this for the guy: he spoke highly of the twins and showed them max respect.

Ron told me of the day when Harry lost the plot and shot in the office with a bucket full of shit and let them all have it! He got a terrible kicking over that, but Ron said he was laughing all the way to the choky as they dragged him off the wing! I think Harry lived all his life on the edge. He had been brutalised throughout his time inside, but that was just normal to him. That's how sick jail can be. It can often turn men into animals, it breeds desperation.

I never did see Harry again – he was in his forties then, so he's got to be over seventy today. But I've never forgotten him, and later the twins spoke of him with respect. So it was mutual. If anyone knows what happened to him, let me know. I've met some legends in my time! Really, I class myself as very lucky to have met so many.

The twins were never too keen on the IRA, and they kept well clear of them. But I've got to say now, they're good lads to have on your side in jail – I mean loyal, fearless and very solid – unlike the Kray henchmen, most of whom turned to shit when the heat was turned up.

I don't like what the IRA do outside; some are fucking heartless evil bastards! But, inside, I've never really had any trouble with them. I've done bird with them all: Roy Walsh, Billy Armstrong, Martin Brady, Sean O'Connell, Vince Downey, Harry Duggan, Paul Wordane, Noel Gibson, Nat Vella (a bit of a slippery fucker him, told lots of lies! I never liked him). Now, Paddy Hackett, he was a hero of mine; he had a leg off and an arm blown clean off! Yeah, a right cripple he was! He was on the blanket for years, what a strong man he was, pure will power, and he even used to go to the gym. Put his stump arm in the hole of the weight and lift! He was serving twenty years and he did them like a true warrior.

Dingus McGhee – Dingus was on a two-year shit-up (if you don't know what a shit-up is, buy my *Good Prison Guide* book, and you'll learn prison talk from that), and he escaped off the Whitemoor unit! A true rebel, and I loved the guy! Dingus never liked the bombers, he was a triggerman – blow your brains out!

Yeah, I met 'em all, and most of 'em I admired! Any riots and they were there in the thick of it; any protests and they backed you! So I can't now, nor ever, knock 'em.

There were the odd few I despised. Well, you can't get on with the whole world, can you? You've got to fight some people or we will all end up hippies and flower power people, peace and love and all that shit!

Who needs that? It's pathetic, next we will be playing catchy kissy and making daisy chains. Give me an axe any day!

* * * * *

It was back in 1976 that I first bumped into the twins. I landed in Parkhurst Jail on the Isle of Wight, a 24-year-old man serving time for armed robbery and violence – even back then I was labelled one of Britain's most violent men!

I had been sentenced at Chester Crown Court in 1974 for a total of 28 years, though fortunately it was all to run concurrently, so in reality I ended up with seven years.

From 1974 to 1976, I had been moved to all the worst dungeons in the penal system: Waterloo, Leeds, Liverpool, Wandsworth, Hull, Durham, the list goes on and on. All had a bit of me!

In the space of two years, I had built up a record of over twenty attacks on screws. Prison and me never married – it was a courtship of isolation and pain. It made me worse. I never liked it – and it never liked me. Not a week went by that I wasn't jumped on and beaten up; I was in and out of strong boxes and strip cells like a jack in a box. Straightjackets, body belts, even injections.

So, in 1976 I land in Parkhurst. To give you an idea of what 'The Big House' – the number-one jail at that time, which housed the monarchs of the villain world –

was really like, I'll say that it was full of men you didn't fuck with! Hard men! Fearless! Men I admire, real men, not like the maggots of today. Men who never needed drugs to survive. Men who lived with high morals and self-respect. Real criminals. Great armed robbers, the best, like Joey Martin, Siddy Draper, Danny Alpress, Billy Gentry, Ronnie Easterbrook, Roy Shaw, Tommy Wisbey and Bruce Reynolds.

There were the cop killers: Harry Roberts, Freddie Sewell and Billy Skindle. (He was a funny fucker, Billy – he used to say his gun had an iffy trigger, and he never meant to do it. But the cop had seven bullets in him ...) I came into contact with what I rate as some of the most violent men I ever met. One blew a cop away up in Leeds, but while in jail he was a complete psycho! I loved him. Once, in Broadmoor, he ripped into a lunatic with a china mug and tore out a kidney! Real Hannibal Lecter stuff (though he never ate it).

Parkhurst was oozing with excitement – there were psychos, lunatics and terrorists! There were sieges, violence and even murders!

On my first night there, I smashed my cell up and ended up in the strong box. Yeah, my first ever night in Parkhurst was in the double-door box! Sleeping with the cockroaches. Armies of them marched in; my body was a mass of bruises and cuts, but my heart was strong, my mind even stronger. Violence becomes a way of life. You learn to become it, you learn to accept the life they force you to live; they create what you are!

The next day, Dr Cooper saw me. He was the PMO (Psychiatric Medical Officer) who was to become the catalyst to my friendship with the twins. I was put on to C Unit, which was known throughout the system as 'Cooper's Troopers' Nutters Wing. This was a psychiatric wing – everyone on it was considered to be either insane or very unpredictable.

I remember Wally – now, Wally was a big strong Geordie and had once taken a screw hostage. He had also been to Rampton Asylum for the criminally insane. Nobody messed with Wally. He was fourteen stone of energy. At times he exploded just to release his frustrations. When that happened, it would take twenty screws to subdue him – along with a strong tranquilliser.

Then there was Dougie. Dougie killed outside then killed inside (he strangled a lifer). He also took hostages; Doug was a very volatile sort of guy! A big Leeds man, with a big heart and awesome strength.

There was Billy, a Birmingham armed robber. He seemed like a normal guy, but, when he got upset, he was lethal, like the day he smashed into a con with a flask. Crash!

Colin was ex-Broadmoor – he caved a con's head in with a rock and cut up several more. Colin had killed outside and nearly killed inside many times. He suffered from bad depression and used to swallow objects – razor blades, bed springs etc., and they would take him outside for operations. Colin ended up a life-long pal. At times I prayed for this guy, simply because I felt so much sadness for him and what he was putting himself through – the pain, the misery of it all. But that's prison in a nutshell: pain.

Chilly Chamberlain came from my hometown of Luton. Chilly lost the plot years ago because of drugs. He's a pill head and a smack head. He never knew what day it was. Once, he walked into my cell and said, 'What time's the bus due?' He was off his head, crazy. He was on another planet!

Oh, and there was Mad Jacko. This guy was the biggest problem the system ever had; always up to something, any way to fuck the system: a rooftop siege, a shit-up. Violence. Hunger strikes. A hostage. Very unpredictable.

Now do you get the picture? Now do you see what C-wing was? It never had more than a dozen prisoners on it, all of them had a problem and most of them were mad (or nearly mad). All had the same thing in common; we were trapped up in the bowels of the system.

But the two cons who kept that wing alive, made it a better place to be, were the twins, Ronnie and Reggie!

They moved on to the wing in 1972, from an SSU (Special Security Unit), so they were settled by the time I moved in there. The day before I arrived there, Dr Cooper had pulled them in the office and told them I was coming, and that I was very volatile. They were asked if they would try to calm me down, and help me settle! Ronnie told me later that he'd said to Dr Cooper, 'I'm not a fucking welfare officer.'

From the moment I walked on to C-wing, I felt strangeness overcome me (no jail wing had ever had this effect on me before). It was like walking on a graveyard. Eerie! I could sense and smell madness; it was like walking through a minefield, waiting to be blown up. I was more alert than ever before. Not fearful, but more on my toes. Excited!

The first con I saw was Colin Robinson. He was leaning over the rails, up on landing '2'. Our eyes met. Now Colin won't mind me saying this, but his eyes are the sort you see in horror films: bulging, mad and dangerous.

He shouted down to me, 'Cuppa tea, mate?'

'Yeah, nice, cheers, pal.'

The screws took me to my cell. It was clean! Cleaner than what I was used to, owing to my long periods of punishment. Colin walked in, we shook hands and he passed me my mug of tea! It was sweet! I hadn't had a cup of tea like this for ages, and it tasted lovely.

Colin sat on the bed, I sat on the chair, we had a chat. I knew from that point we would be special pals.

'How long are you doing?' I asked

'Two lives with a rec (-ommendation) of 25 years,' he replied with a grin that would have sent Frankenstein running. He had recently got his second life for cutting up a paedophile in Wakefield. That man had more stitches in him than a mailbag. I noticed Colin's arms were full of self-inflicted scars; he was a very sad case. I felt a lot of compassion for him; he had serious bouts of depression, brought on by despair and doubt.

A tap came on the door – and it opened! In walked this guy with a jug of coffee and a packet of chocolate biscuits. (I hadn't seen a chocolate biscuit for months and months.) He put them down on the table and put his hand out, 'I'm Reg Kray, nice to meet you.'

Obviously, by now I knew all about the Krays. I had even met some of the Firm in the other jails – and also some of their enemies! But meeting Reg Kray, for me, was like meeting royalty; I stood up and shook his hand!

Reg told me he had heard all about me from one of his pals, Harry Johnson. He had told them all about me up in Hull Jail, when I wreaked havoc on the place! Reg told me to box it clever and settle down, try and do my time easy. He was pleased I was there and said he would train with me in the gym! After five minutes or so, he left.

Colin said, 'Great guy is Reg, the best!'

Colin left and I was sorting my cell out when there was another tap on the door. In walked Reg again, with a battery record player and a good twenty LPs! He put them down and stuck his hand out. 'Hi, I'm Ronnie Kray.' (Well, he was dressed the same as Reg, so at the time I thought it *was* Reg … ha, ha.) Ron was to end up the greatest friend I ever had. From the moment we shook hands and our eyes met, I knew this was no ordinary guy.

Yes, Ron was mad – you could see the madness in his eyes – but not mad in the sense of 'out of control'. He was just mad, fearless mad, nobody or nothing stopped

Ronnie Kray. When he was on a mission, he could not be stopped. Ron was the only man to ever make me stop and think. His whole being was unique; he had an aura, he oozed power, but he had an amazing way of making people aware. He never (or only rarely) raised his voice – he spoke very calmly, always saying 'please' and 'thank you', but the moment you fucked with him, his face would change! Those eyes went jet black, and it was like looking into no-man's-land! That smirk would take over. Violence wasn't very far away.

Ronnie hated, despised and loathed liberty-takers and bullies! When he walked out of my cell, I sat and looked at the LPs. Every one was signed to the twins: The Small Faces, Cliff Richard, Shirley Bassey, Timi Yuro, Dean Martin, Peters & Lee, Matt Monro! Ron had loaned me his prize collection. I was honoured!

I had just met two icons! And on that first meeting with Ron, he said something to me that I have never forgotten: 'Doing time is easy,' he said. 'The hard bit is the rats and slags you've got to do it with!' I've never forgotten that. It's so fucking true.

That night, I played the Timi Yuro LP. Until then I had never heard of her, but she became one of my all-time favourites. My favourite song by Timi is 'Hurt' – it's awesome! She's French – and what a voice! Now, it's no secret that I love the girl from Tiger Bay, Shirley Bassey. Well, believe it or not, I went out with Shirley Bassey! OK, not the star, a Shirley at my school, Icknield High, in Luton! But she had the same name! My claim to fame, ha, ha. The real Shirley Bassey is my all-time singer, but Timi Yuro comes a close second· When she sings 'Hurt', my skin goes all sensitive.

So there I was all tucked up in my cosy bed! Lights out! In my high-security cell all alone with Timi Yuro, and a wing full of killers and dangerous psychos! Who said there ain't a heaven? I was in heaven! Chocolate biscuits from Reggie and Timi Yuro courtesy of Ronnie and a nice warm bed. Good friends! Such a shame it never stays peaceful! When the door is shut, we are all in our own dreams; behind every door there is a dream.

Sadly, most of our dreams are shattered and destroyed; in the dark of the night there will be a scream or a shout, some dream turned into a nightmare! We can't escape it, it becomes a 'lifemare', but we have to get on with it – survive. In the morning the door is unlocked. A new day … or is it?

I've had years of prison life, and I believe it affects prisoners without us realising it. I'll try to explain why. People outside read or see the news on TV about some crazed axe murderer and picture him as a rabid dog, but, in jail, he is just a next-door neighbour, a number, a fellow convict. If he doesn't mess with me, who gives a fuck? Anyway, he hasn't got his axe!

I've met 'em all, the meanest fuckers in your worst nightmares, and most are not what you expect. Take Donald Nielsen, for instance, the Black Panther. So how do you picture him? This killer is about 5ft 4in tall, weighs ten stone and has a soft voice. Personally I despise the rat – his cell smells, he is a scruffy maggot and a disgrace to the human race.

Archie Hall, the mad butler. Another five-times killer. They come no more evil than him, eyes like owls, always watching! The only thing that kept him going was getting his dick sucked!

Then there is Bamber, another five-times killer. Innocent Bamber, poor old Jeremy ... He's about as innocent as Al Capone was! It makes me laugh, it really does, if they had just hanged the bastard fifteen years ago we could have forgotten all about the slag! It's amazing how many women write to him! They should take a look at the holes he put into his five victims – two of them kids. Any woman who's got the hots for a child killer is a witch, a Myra Hindley incarnate.

Straffen! Now he's got to be the most evil geezer I've met! An old man now, he's served fifty years. Strangled three little girls. He is still a Cat A, and he will die a Cat A. (For those of you who don't know, Cat A means you, as a prisoner, are considered to be a 'high risk' and 'a danger to the public'.) What a waste of taxpayers' money, keeping him alive for fifty years. He was originally sentenced to death, but he got reprieved.

I once slung a bucket of shit all over him in Long Lartin Prison! He stood there covered in turds, with that sad-eyed look of his. (I wish I had a photo of it.) He was too old to chin! So I just spat on him and threw shit in his cell to make life hell for the slag. My skin crawls when his sort are near me. I just picture the kids they did in, and it upsets me.

Take that Fletcher, who raped and killed a baby. He was on C Unit in the 1970s. One day, it was planned to serve him up 'big time'. We could just not accept such filth in our face; it was time to destroy the cunt! So, I got a tool – I made it from the handle of a Fidelity radio. It was eighteen inches long, and I sharpened it up. The plan was to stab him in the ear and push it into his brain. The twins liked the plan; they just said to be careful! But, for some reason, the authorities moved the slag! He must have got worried; very lucky, he was. In the Seventies I was forever serving the fuckers up. I was on a mission!

The Cambridge Rapist, Peter Cook, got ten life sentences in the 1970s. I bumped into him in Parkhurst in 1976. Our paths crossed one night while on association. I got over to A Wing to see a pal (a one-off) – we had some biz to sort out – when I spotted Cook. You could not miss him; the slag was a transvestite! I blame the screws for allowing it to go on. He had these black satin skirts (skin tight), lipstick and that fucking stupid 'come and get me, boys' walk! I went for him, dragged him in the recess and beat the shit out of him. I used him as a punch bag. Every punch I gave him, I felt as though I was doing it for the ten girls he abused. He'd done terrible things to them girls – up the bum, all sorts of evil degradation! Yeah, I've met 'em all!

Vicky Miller! Raped 25 boys, killed one – he's serving natural life. Dirty fucking rat! Back in 2000, I attempted to smash his cell door in – why? 'Cos I wanted to smash his fat ugly face in! Forty fucking screws jumped me; I was bent up, wrapped up and slung in a van! Miller is a fucking dog! He deserves to be smashed up every day of his life, and the cunt's got a TV in his cell. He's got a bed and a window, and I've got a piss pot and fuck all!

People like Miller should be topped! There is no excuse for his crimes, only evil! You won't believe this, but, when Miller was in Full Sutton Jail, he used to give cons tobacco for their soiled underpants. He gets his rocks off from sniffing underpants! Don't it make you wanna puke up!

Another child slayer is Lennie Smith, 6ft 4in of him, and eighteen stone. I met this beast in Parkhurst Wing in 1985/86. He was a bully – used his size to intimidate. I caught the beast in the bathhouse getting sucked off by a con who was terrified of him. I picked up the mop bucket and smashed his ugly face in. The lad pleaded with me not to say what I saw – what can you do! It stinks, but then that's prison. Filth like Smith should be killed off!

The Guernsey Beast, Beasley, you'll remember this rat! He got thirty years for buggery on boys; he held the island of Guernsey in fear! Well, sadly, I could not get to this slag, but I did once squirt him with piss from a shampoo bottle through my cell window as he passed it to go to work at Albany, I drenched him. He served twenty years and got out.

Then there was Morris, the Cannock Chase killer,

another rat. He's served about 35 years now (hopefully, he will die in jail) I slung a PP9 (large square battery) battery at him, got him bang smack in the face (should have been a grenade).

What about Mad Patel, the Pakistani beast? You'll love this, the reptile kidnapped two boys! Tortured them, had sex with them, but he came unstuck big time in prison: he got a broom rammed up his arse in Parkhurst and had his throat slit! (Survived it, sadly.) But he now has to wear incontinence pants ... nappies! He walks like one of those puppets in *Thunderbirds*! (Better than death, though, eh?) That's what all the beasts should get – a broom up the arse – but it's you, the taxpayers, keeping them alive!

Barry Williams! He shot dead five innocent people, and was sent to Broadmoor forever. Ron used to say, 'Watch him, he a right rat!'

Mark Rowntree was another, killed five (two were kids). And he doesn't even know why he did it!

One geezer in Broadmoor killed and cut up a woman and sent her tits in a parcel to a national paper! Why? So he could be famous! You can't make this shit up!

Imagine Ronnie Kray having to live with such madness for all those years. Think of all those psychotics with voices in their heads saying 'attack'. Men have died for no reason in prison, just for looking at a rat the wrong way. Those psychos will rip your eyes out – that's why the screws make certain their nails are kept short. Barry Quiggly was a classic psychotic, he was forever jumping on people and biting them. (They removed his teeth in the end, to stop him doing it!)

But let's not forget the screws' games as well, the way they endlessly wind people up. Some of them deserved all they got – a big scar to remind them not to fuck with people! There were plenty of psychotics in jail as well; a lot of these guys have serious problems! But they're too dangerous to be hospitalised.

One I know (who will remain nameless) is the most complicated man I know. A pain freak. No man alive could stop him; I've seen him steam into a dozen screws just to get to the one he wants! They've smashed him to a pulp ... injected him so many times, it's now useless – there is no cure!

I never cried when I got stabbed or cut or smashed up by a dozen screws. Screws are bullies and cowards (in three decades they've only ever beaten me in mobs). They are rats, vultures, stick and boot men. They've even beaten me when I'm wrapped up in a body belt ... brave fuckers! I've beaten them face to face, eye to eye, fist in face! That's me. All you nonces and grasses, I'll creep up on you and slice you up and laugh! I've been accused of so many things. I smile and say, 'Prove it!' I'm not daft enough to say, 'Yeah, I did that cunt,' am I? Many are best forgotten. (Well, not forgotten... kept as a nice memory.)

Years ago, in prison, it was commonplace for cons to carry a cut-throat in the picture show, or for a big weight to mysteriously be dropped on someone's head in the gym or for there to be a stabbing in the shower. All those suicides … do you believe they were all really suicides? Do me a favour, get real! Men are often killed in jail. That's how it is. If ever I die mysteriously then it will be murder, as I have no death wish! I was once dragged out of bed in the middle of the night – a good ten screws steamed in, all in masks and gloves. I was in the block as they dragged me out of the cell. They held me up, and a noose was hanging from a beam.

'Fuck in our jail, Bronson, and that's for you. We will make it look like suicide.'

Next day, I slung a pot full of shit at a screw! Why? 'Cos I then felt safe! As I told the governor, I did it 'cos I'm in fear of my life! (I was moved within hours.)

Yeah, if yours truly ever dies mysteriously, don't ever believe I took my own life! 'Cos these fuckers will have done me in. Drugs, poison or whatever! The system destroyed me!

American mobsters would laugh at it over here, it's a fucking joke. Faces, chaps, doing the screws' work! Any of the max-secure lads will tell you! They see it every day, so-called faces grovelling for parole.

The real chaps know who they are and they know I'm spot on! And, at the end of the day, who's ever gonna serve their life like I have? Can you survive 24 years in solitary? I've served longer than Norman Parker and he killed two people; he probably spent a couple of years in solitary at the most – a big-time rebel! I've done that sitting on the pot and so have other true solitary men who have given up years and years of their life to fight the corrupt system. I'll name them, men I admire:

John Bowden: years of struggle. John took a governor hostage in Parkhurst, a top man! Bob Maudsley: twenty-plus years of solitary! OK, Bob's mad, but he has more bottle in one toe than most have in their whole body! Mad Jacko, Wally Lee, Frank Fraser, Marty Frape, Timmy Noonan, Steve Lannigan, Roy Walsh, Noel Gibson, Paddy Hill and Kevin Brown.

The twins had the gift of weighing up people. Sadly I've not got it, so I have to face a lot of adversity on my journey through hell and find myself in difficult situations, let down by people I thought were my pals. Like Ginger Evans: he came in to my cell up in Full Sutton, told me a pack of lies, and I helped him out! Paid off his debt, I had to chin a guy for him, had to get back his radio and watch, then he vanishes, puts himself on protection, he owed everybody! The cunt used me to make him right! I pray I meet up with him again, and many others like him!! You can't help some people. Reg Kray's favourite saying was, 'You can't help nobody who won't help themselves', and those are such true words.

* * * * *

Recently, I received a letter from Kate Kray, thanking me for the cartoon of mine that sold at a charity auction, it raised £180. It was A4 size and took me twenty minutes to complete! That works out to £540 per hour! And I'm mad? Yeah, well, I'll be mad all day for that!

My cartoon was the second highest value item sold! A Manchester United football shirt (signed) sold for £240. So there you have it. I still help raise cash for the kids in this hole, and it's that sort of thing that makes me feel a better man! Nobody on this planet can take that away from me! And it's these things that never get told, so I'm telling you, 'cos it's fucking time people saw me in a different light! So up yours, Jack Straw! I sleep at peace! Do you? What's the man of Straw ever done? Let Reg out to die? Big deal! What a heart! We'll probably find Myra Hindley living in a secret location 'cos her death was faked just to release her, see what they can do for such filth. And, yet, people like Reggie are left to rot!

I passed Madame Tussaud's on the way to the appeal courts. I went there when I was a kid, and loved it – especially the chamber of horrors. I hear the twins are in there – see, they live on and they always will. Icons. I bet Jack Straw never makes it there after he's dead. How can we forget them? Be honest, we can't!

Ron once said, 'More people have heard of us than The Beatles.' And he told his trial judge Melford Stevenson, 'If I wasn't here, I'd be having a drink with Judy Garland!' That's Ron – style. You can't take it away from him! He was the guv'nor! I loved it when he came out with those sayings; he used to do it to the screws a lot. But he had a way of doing it that only he could carry off. Half the time, even the screws never realised till half an hour later that he had mugged them off! He'd walk away with a grin!

The Colson brothers (Peter and Tony) are a similar breed – very witty, very clever. Two good robbers who know how to manipulate the system. Top men! Another good family of top villains are the Anslow Brothers, Dave, Eric and John, known as the Dudley firm. I met them in the early Seventies in Parkhurst. Great guys, they just don't make robbers like them any more. John recently lost a leg (but he is still more of a man than the mugs who call themselves criminals today). Good villains are rare these days. Gangsters are even rarer! Even today's hit men are weak. Something has gone desperately wrong ... why? You tell me.

Look at all the gangsters up in Manchester! What's that all about? Poxy drugs. Crack city! Who needs it? I don't, nor will I get involved!

But if it ever hits me in the face, I swear, I'll go on a mission to clean up the streets! Instead of using a broom, I'll be a sweeper of the bodies, the 'filth disposer'. They are scum, soul suckers, drug mugs and spineless cockroaches.

After all the bird I've done, you would think I'd have got a TV. Well, I hardly ever get one, but I hear all the monsters have one! Your Bradys; your Millers; your Rippers! (Oh yeah, 24-inch colour TV sets for them.)

But your Bronsons and Frasers don't get such comfort; we have to make do with our own entertainment.

Solitary is no joke; it's a soulless existence, but it's a good test of a man's character. I'd say it's similar to a gun pointing in your face: do you shit or do you smile, do you beg or do you pray? Only you know what to do, if or when it happens. When the steel door slams up, and you're alone, and you know it's for years, only then you realise what true solitary means. Now it's all I really know. I really don't know any other way! To use a famous phrase, I am now a 'product of the system'. For me it's natural, Billy of the Beast syndrome: survive or die!

But when I think of the slags watching TV in a nice cosy cell, all mod cons, it does upset me! Paedophiles watching kids' films, rapists watching sex films, psychos watching horror films ... then there's me watching a cockroach scuttle across the floor, or seeing a spider spin a web, while those slags get off on their movies!

So does crime pay? Does it? How many criminals ever really win? Take Ronnie Biggs! He spent 36 years on the run, now he's at death's door. Where is he now? In a stinking cell – in hell before he gets there!

All the young kids who think crime's a good thing should just go look into Ronnie Biggs' eyes! He is a sad old man, dying a lonely death; fuck knows why he ever flew back to the UK.

Me, I'd rather have stuck a gun in my mouth than return to prison! Ronnie Biggs must have had his reasons, but I'll say now he won't get any favours off prison H/Q or any compassion off the big boys up there in Whitehall! He will die a very sad old man. A prison death is the loneliest death on earth.

While I'm at it, let me give you the facts of all the great train robbers, all Ronnie Biggs' pals. Then you can work out for yourself whether crime pays!

Buster Edwards: he got 25 years for his part in the great train robbery, and served nine years. He opened his little flower stall and seemed to be happy ... but was he? 'Cos in 1994, he hanged himself.

Charlie Wilson. He copped thirty years for it, like Ronnie Biggs. He escaped and made it to Canada, where he was nicked and brought back. He served ten years and got out. In 1994, at his house 'Chequers' in Marbella, he was shot dead.

Roy James. He served twelve years of a thirty-year sentence. Roy was a top-class racing driver; he ruined a great career. Then in 1993, he shot his father-in-law and got a six-year prison sentence. He died in 1997.

Brian Field. Now this geezer was a solicitor, but he got mixed up in crime and got a lump of bird. He served six years. Some ten years later, he died in a motor accident.

Robert Welch was given thirty years, but was released in 1976. He's now a cripple, after a leg operation that went badly wrong.

William Boal. This guy made it to 1970. He never got released – well he did, in a body bag! A brain tumour took him out, so his sentence was death!

Bruce Reynolds. He served twenty years of a 25 stretch, and is now a successful author! Tommy Wisbey had some bad luck. He got thirty years, got out in 1976, but came back in for ten years in 1989. Gordon Goody got out in 1975 after being given thirty years. James Hassey, like Gordon Goody, was given thirty years. He got out in 1975 but came back in 1989 for seven years. Roger Cordrey got twenty years. James White ... eighteen years. Leonard Field ... 25 yrs. John Wheater ... three years – he got a three-year stretch just for perverting the course of justice!

So add it all up, did these guys win? Did the Krays win? Did any fucker win? How can you win? One fucking day of bird is a waste! You lose right from the first day you walk in, or get slung in! We are all losers in our own way!

Ronnie Biggs is now sleeping in despair, waiting to die! One day he was in Rio with the sun, sea and sex, now he has fuck all but a window with bars. That's what you call lost! A lost soul!

So give it a lot of serious thought, the glamour doesn't last, every party has to come to a stop! Nothing goes on! It's got to end; you can only push your luck so far, then it's over!

It's like the lion tamer: 100 times he will put his head in the lion's mouth, 100 times the crowd will cheer! Then, on the 101st time, the cheers turn to screams. It can't all be sweet, it's got to end some time. You chance life, you can't always win! Like Evel Knievel, Eddie Kidd and Muhammad Ali, anybody up the top has to crash. It's the same with criminals: ninety per cent of criminals never even reach the top. They're born to lose.

I've seen death, dead eyes and old men shuffling around a prison exercise yard. I've seen it, smelled it and it's not nice to see! Take John Buddy the cop killer. John was a proud man; he had a lot of self-respect, and everyone liked him (apart from the pigs, that is), but look at his end! His heart gave up on him in Parkhurst. He never got the best of treatment – why should he, he was a cop killer in the system's eyes. Who cared if he lived or died? So he died!

I watched old Bishy die, an old lifer! Bishy was a lovely old boy; he got life over an arson attack. He had this thing about fire! But it cost him thirty years of this shit; he died in Parkhurst too!

One old lifer dropped down dead in front of me in the exercise yard – I'll never forget it, you can't forget such things. He just gave up on living. I looked at the guy next to me and said, 'I'll have his dinner.' It was a joke, but deep down I was sad.

Life can be death inside, we are all facing death – the stress, the strain and the anxiety and the never knowing. I learned from all the death to go on and win. I see every day as a challenge. The same was to be said of Reggie and Ronnie, they tried and they lost … I aim to carry their flag for them and be a winner.

I saw a young con hanging up in Risley back in 1970. That sight has remained with me – the bulging eyes, the swollen blue tongue, the cold marble look and the smell of shit! I was just a lad myself. This boy was only seventeen years old. He had been put in for nicking a car and he just gave up on life.

I've seen 'em cut their throats, wrists and one lunatic even sliced his dick off in Broadmoor! Life is precious, but some people don't want to go on.

Some birds in cages die after a while, only 'cos they can't fly. They don't want to be in a cage – why the fuck should they be caged?

Talking of birds, let me put something straight. Some years back, it said in the press that I ate a fellow con's budgie! Well, the truth is … I never! Nor would I ever do such a thing. I love birds! But, having said that, I must admit I did once lose my head and pull a budgie's head off! It was up in Hull Jail, in 1975. My next-door neighbour had a budgie and every morning at 6am the fucker would sing. It drove me nuts! I pulled the con: 'Look, mate, be reasonable, it's upsetting me.' He got lemon with me. As if it was my fault! So I waited for the next day to come. It started up; I got up and just went fucking mad! When the doors unlocked, I steamed in to his pad. I hit him so hard I thought I killed him, then I grabbed the bird and ripped its head off! Amazing – so much blood from such a little head!

Well, that guy had a breakdown! He had had that bird for five years, it was the greatest thing in his life, and he was a lifer! I felt so fucking bad, I mean bad. I felt hate towards myself for what I had done. I learned a lot that day. I got him a new bird sent in, but it was never the same for the guy. I killed his best friend.

I couldn't take it any more ... I was full of guilt, so I went into his cell (after his spell in the hospital wing) and pulled out a sauce bottle.

He covered up. 'No, it's OK mate,' I told him. 'I'm not going to hurt you, you're gonna hurt me.'

'What!' He was in shock.

I handed him the bottle. 'Go on ... smash it into my head, rip up my face!'

'Why?'

''Cos I said so.'

'I can't do that,' he said.

So I took the bottle off him and smashed it over my head.

I gave it back to him. 'Go on, ram it in my body, in my face and chop me up!'

Do you know what? He wouldn't do it, he couldn't do it! If he had killed my best friend, I'd have rammed it up his arse so far it would have pierced his heart!

He moved back over to the hospital wing after that and told the governor I was insane! Yeah, I've seen a lot of prison hell and it's not nice!

* * * * *

There was a right old flash screw in Parkhurst in '76. He was in the Parkhurst '69 riot and gave out a lot of stick. I remember one day, he got lemon with Ron Kray. Ron's face went purple! Ron slagged him off and then went and slammed up! I saw the slag grinning, so I went up to him and spat in his face – that stopped him from grinning! He nicked me. I think I got fourteen days. So I then scalded the slag! We never saw him again after that. Ron was made up; we had a party over that!

I'd say nine out of ten screws at Parkhurst treated the twins with respect, but there was always the odd slag. You could always smell it. The atmosphere of evil. Some screws try to make a name for themselves – 'I nicked Kray', 'I kicked Bronson in the balls'. It happens in all walks of life, but a guy don't have to accept it!

At the end of the day the twins helped keep the unit calm and easy. They defused a lot of incidents. Like the time I had a fall-out with Davey Simmonds. I won't slag the guy – fall-outs happen! So we had words in the gym. I got very sick in the head, and I wanted to hurt him there and then – but Reggie stopped it. Davey left.

I said to Reg, 'He's gotta have some!'

Reg said, 'No tools!'

So I followed him into his cell and we had it off. It was a fist fight, but I got carried away. I started smashing him with a table leg that came off as we fell on it! It was Reg and Ron who steamed in and pulled me off! Davey was in a right mess, but, respect to him, he took it! But I never trusted him after that! Would you? He was doing twenty years!

Yeah, the twins were a great help to us all on C Wing. There would have been murders on there without them, or riots! It's insane – I'm looking back 25 years, but it's like last week to me!

Canteen days were special to us – we always got a treat. The twins would get some 'civvy' fags, a change from their roll-ups! I'd get some drinking chocolate or a chocolate gateaux or even a cheesecake. I'd treat the lads! I used to eat mine out on the landing, just so the screws could watch me, each mouthful, and I'd smile at the rats. That's how to win! Eat well and live good! Occasionally, I would buy some cigars, just so the lads could smoke them in front of the screws!

I used to like to wear a new T-shirt, new trainers and feel good. If you dress good, you feel good, if you feel good, you are good! Screws like to put us down – make us wear rags 'cos a lot of them are jealous fuckers, envious.

I remember Danny Alpress. He was a top robber and they were gutted over his lifestyle in Parkhurst. Even his visitors pulled up in Rolls-Royces! Screws hate all that. They can't accept it that some of us have earned more in one blag than they earn in years. That upsets them, which is why you get so many corrupt ones! It's no good denying it, it's fact!

CHAPTER 3

PARKHURST TRUTHS

Ron Kray's cell was called the 'Blue Lagoon', and was done out like a little club. Parkhurst cells are the old type: long and cosy, not like the rat holes today! Ron had his cell carpeted, he had curtains, a blue lampshade and all his photos on the walls. Photos of boxers, singers, actors, gangsters and family. He also had a large Persian rug with a tiger on it. There was a bed with a tiger bedspread, and he had two lockers, a table and a soft chair.

When you were in Ron's cell, you weren't in prison, you were in a club. There was always the odd bottle of vodka in a plastic bottle, which he mixed with prison hooch! Even in jail, the twins knew how to live. Little lords!

Ron would be relaxed, friendly and always great company; he always kept himself immaculately dressed and spotless (self-respect)! Even in prison clothes he looked special, with his starched shirts and shiny shoes.

Nobody walked in Ron's cell without being invited in. Roy Grantham was one who thought he could. He got a bottle rammed in his face, and the twins cut him to pieces! He was an ignorant sod, a prison bully and a slag!

We would sit in the Blue Lagoon just passing time, having a chat, a drink and a laugh. I'll say now before I go on, Ron was special to me (as you've probably already gathered by now). I was closer to Ron than I was to Reg, simply because we both suffered with mental illness. Ron was a paranoid schizophrenic and I was, or I am, a very complicated man (as I'll explain later). But Ron had this strange way about him – he could read my mind and he knew when I was not myself. He just knew when I was about to blow up.

One time I was in his company along with Reg, Cubby and this big fat slob called Pete Murray, who was a Jock. I had the urge to punch his fat face; he just got on my nerves! I never liked him; in fact, I despised him. Ron sensed it and all of a sudden, he asked Murray and Cubby to leave his cell. Even Reg looked stunned.

'OK, what's up?' Ron asked.

I told him, 'It's that big fat slag. I don't like him!'

'Why?' he asked me.

''Cos he's a slimy fucker,' I said.

'What's he done to you?'

'Nothing yet, but I sense he will. I don't trust him.'

42

Then Ron said, 'I don't trust him either,' and Reg said, 'Wc only use him as a carrier!'

Ron called them back in, but Cubby stayed out for some reason.

'OK, tell him.'

So I told Murray, 'I don't like you!'

He looked at Ron and then Reg and said, 'What's up?'

I said, 'You're a rat and I can see straight through you!'

After that, he was paranoid. Days later, I hit him in the gym with the mop bucket, sparked him out! Reg witnessed it and smiled! Soon after, he disappeared, moved off!

Years later, he got out and murdered two young boys up in Manchester and got natural life! Jock Murray! So my instinct was spot on! A rat – eighteen stone of shit. Reg loved it and so did Ron when he got told!

I used to work out with Reg. He was fit and fast, it was a privilege to watch him on the punch bag – at this time they had only served eight years. They ate well and trained well – well, Reg did, not so much Ron.

Me and Reg would do a lot of sparring. Often he caught me some awesome body shots. Once I caught him right on the chin – he buckled, but Reg loved it, he was a natural! It's really tragic, as he could have been a champion boxer, he was a controlled fighter, and he kept his cool. His footwork and combinations were second to none!

He taught me how to bob and weave, duck and dive – a moving target is harder to hit! I used to enjoy our workouts and so did he. Often, Ron would come in with a mug of tea and sit and watch us! Sometimes he would join in on the sit-ups, but Reg was dedicated, he loved it!

At this time, I was a bundle of energy. I could not keep still for five minutes, I had to work it out of me. It was during one workout with Reg that Chilly Chamberlain upset me. I have known Chilly since I was a schoolboy; he is a good lad, a bit crazy but a good pal to have. But that day he came in the gym smoking and coughing all over the place, then he got in the way and just upset me.

I picked him up and threw him, and he crashed into the wall unconscious. I thought I had killed him, a screw ran in and the bells went, but thankfully he came round. I felt terrible for days after, so I finally said sorry and cooked him a meal and we were pals again! The screw dropped us out, as screws go they were laid-back, but there is always one who is never happy unless there is some action! The trouble-shooters I call them – brainless wankers!

Bernie Dixon was doing a ten stretch and in 1976 he came on to C Unit, Parkhurst. Nobody liked him, least of all me. Ron hated his guts. It was his whole attitude. Done it! Got it! Know it all! He was a good fifteen years older and I just knew he was trouble to me.

It happened in our little kitchen. I was in there with

Chilly. Dixon came in and there was some bother. I remember the day well: it was a day I never really wanted any aggro because I had a visit with my mum and dad; you have to think of your parents every time. So I tried to let it go, but he was coming on strong.

Even Chilly could sense the vibes and he was forever out of his skull. It was just one of those incidents that could not be switched off. It had to happen.

These wooden rolling pins don't half come in handy. The next thing I remember, both the twins and Chilly were on me. It was like a dream, or a nightmare. We all got banged up, but Dixon got moved (well, carried) over to the hospital wing.

When my door opened after dinner, I thought, I am off. That's fucked my visit. But, as luck would have it, I was called for my visit. It so happened that Mad Taffy Hughes was on a visit at the same time. Taffy helped the orderly over in the hospital. He told me Dixon was in a bad way. I said aloud, 'Tell him when he is better to come back and have some more.' I suppose the moral of the story is simple, how many people can say that the twins jumped them but they never got a scratch? Looking back, I am grateful they did – they saved me from a life sentence.

Dixon later got out, ended up on another armed robbery and got fourteen years. Some people never learn, do they?

Chilly used to do all the flasks for bang up. He would fill them up and put them in each cell. Now Ron loved his cup of char, nobody drank tea like the Colonel, so he always had two flasks. I am talking big flasks. Each flask was like three big mugs, so that is six fucking pints of tea!

That night, for some reason, Chilly left Ron out – why or how it is beyond me. Ron banged up at 9pm prompt, as we all did. By about 10pm he was stomping and screaming abuse and banging his door: 'Where are my fucking flasks?'

The night clocky got over all the security and dogs and sorted it – Ron got his flasks. In the morning, Reg shot into Ron's cell and tried to sort it, and calm it all down. Chilly never left his own cell for a week after that.

It really was a genuine mistake. That is how Chilly is – a pill head. He pops so many, he rattles. We finally convinced Ron it really was a complete mistake, and the black cloud passed.

Chilly used to throw the medicine ball at me as part of my training regime. We used to have some good laughs. One day I caught a mouse and I slipped it into Chilly's bed sheets, and he probably slept with it for a week, but never knew it was there. I always used to give him a bowl of my Luton stew, which was famous. Everyone wanted a bowl of it, but not everyone got it. Some don't deserve it, simple as that. Reg liked my stew; he said it was training grub, proper.

* * * * *

I know the old people of today go on about how the summers were better in their day ... well, I have to agree, they're right. The 1970s summers were hot. We had droughts. Our summers were nothing like today. The one we had when I was on the Isle of Wight was the hottest in my life and it seemed to go on and on. These days we have a week of sun and we think it is a result!

On C Unit, we had a sun trap by a wall, which cut off the gym and the workshop. It was painted white and it just caught the sun. About eight of us used to sit there for a couple of hours a day. We were brown as berries. It was there that Ron used to tell us all the great stories of his travels: the USA, Tunisia, Morocco, etc.

Fucking brilliant tour. He even met Peter O'Toole and David Niven out there. He had a dream, some great magic stories. Ron loved meeting people. What a great ambassador he would have made, or London Mayor. We are stuck with that prat Livingstone when Dave Courtney should have got that job on. In fact, I stood for the post, so did Screaming Lord Sutch, but real people never get accepted in life – you have to be a brown nose.

What they wrote was to me, for me, not to nobody else. The same goes for my mum. She had cards off them for years and years.

Apart from my pocket watch, the rest is my own private stuff, so don't ever ask. Offer me a million bucks, ten million and you will get the same answer: fuck off.

Violet's two sisters were Rose and May, and both Ron and Reg adored them. Their surname was Lee. Old Granddad Lee was a good old fighter, so it must have run in the family genes. Born to fight. Ron used to tell me stories of Granddad Lee – blinding stories! Pure East London classics.

Reg had a serious fiery temper in the early part of his sentence. In one of the units in the early Seventies he was padded up with John Duddy (the co-defendant of Harry Roberts, cop killer). John copped a life with a recommendation of thirty years. He later died on F Wing in Parkhurst.

I don't know why Reg had a fight with him, but Harry Johnson was there, and he told me that Reg really laid into him.

Then Reg had a fight with Pete Hurley. Pete was one of the old-school bank robbers. Proper stuff, a top-class blagger. That too was a good fight. Reg was fast, he would let go a cluster of combinations, but screws always have to press the fucking bells, then pile in and make it worse.

Why can't people accept that fights happen, same as in the forces, same as on a building site or a factory? When you get a lot of men in one place, you will always have fights – it is survival of the fittest.

Patsy Manning was a great pal of Reg from way back in the 1950s, but in Long Lartin, Reg even attacked Patsy. It was at a time when Reg was losing the plot. He got right paranoid in those days. The least thing set him off. Patsy had done fuck all wrong, but Reg had it in his head that he had. So he attacked him.

In this game solicitors come and go, most of them are money-orientated rats, who truly don't give a shit about us people. Take it from me, they are true snakes. So, if you do have a good lawyer, respect him or her because they are one of us. Priceless.

I believe Trevor Linn was the best brief Reg ever had on his case. He worked so hard for him and earned a lot of respect. He was there right till the end for Reg. A truly great lawyer.

It happened on one evening association: 6pm–9pm was our association, and we could do as we liked, within reason. I was playing chess with Colin. This screw walked up and stood over us, watching.

'Er, what's your problem?' I asked.

He just stood there. 'Only watching,' he replied.

I looked at Colin and then at him and said, 'Fuck off.'

He smirked, so I picked the table up and hit him. All hell went off – bells, dogs, dozens of screws bent me up and carried me off to the box. I could hear the lads shouting, 'Leave him alone!' But these things happen. It's life in jail. Once back up on the wing, it's back into the routine!

* * * * *

Now it's no secret that Ron was homosexual. I personally don't give a fuck who is and who isn't as long as it's not my ass being pumped! The whole act of it makes me feel sick! I'm nobody's judge; it just does nothing for me.

Ron was a giver, not a taker, and that's how it is. There was talk in later years that Reg was gay or bisexual. Well, I dispute that! In the 25 years I knew Reg I never saw any proof of it. But claims have been made and since I didn't share his cell 24/7 for 365, I have to let that one go.

Anyway, Ron was one hundred per cent that way, but he never hid it – you knew where you stood with him, and if you were not into that lifestyle, you had no problem off him. Ron never forced it on nobody; he treated people with respect.

Once (and only once) I saw a lifer on his knees giving Ron a blowjob in the shower. The sight put me off my grub that day, made me feel a bit sick, but that's life in jail.

Ron used to take a man to his cell and bang up. After half an hour, he would ring his bell and come out for a shower; the lover boy would go to his cell, probably in shame. One of those fags and me never hit it off. Even more so after I had seen that in the shower. I just saw him as a faggot! A spineless rat! He was in his mid-thirties; he got life for killing a woman. I saw him as dog shit!

The day came when he got lemon with me – very cheeky! He thought he could do it, as he was Ron's bit of meat, but if the truth be known I don't think Ron liked him, he was just a means of relief for Ron. I slipped into his cell and nutted him. I smashed out his teeth (they were false), and they all fell out. His nose was bleeding too. I told him I would fucking kill him if he ever got flash with me again.

Obviously, he told Ron, who called me into the Blue Lagoon.

'Sit down! What's the problem?' He looked concerned.

Reg walked in at this point.

'Look, Ron,' I began, 'he got lemon with me so I nutted him.' Sensing what we were talking about, Reg left again promptly.

Ron said, 'Slow down, go easy, anyway he said you smashed his false teeth. So you have done me a favour!'

'Eh, what do you mean, Ron?'

'Well, no teeth, I'll get a better blowjob now!'

That's Ron in a nutshell – a real sense of humour. Reg did not like the homosexuality bit, and it's no secret he stayed clear of Ron's goings on. In fact, they often argued over it. Reg despised any of Ron's bits of meat. He did not want them anywhere near him, or ever in his cell.

Reggie's cell was more like an ordinary cell – he never had it done up like Ron's. Reg was more into reality prison life. When you sat with Reg for a chat, you got prison talk, or talk about boxing or what he planned to do later. Ron was more in the past, in a dream.

I actually felt sorry for Reg, as I felt he was never cut out for prison, he was just too nice a guy! Ron was unpredictable, dangerous, moody ... insane. Reg was deep, smart and very much into business. One thing they both loved was their mum Violet – and I'm lucky, 'cos I met her! In fact, I met her many times on visits, both in Broadmoor and Parkhurst. She was a lovely lady, very warm-hearted, a typical East Ender, and the twins idolised her.

In all these years right up until she died, she never let her boys down, visiting regularly and providing endless love and support. Once, in Broadmoor Asylum, I was up on the roof and saw her come in to visit Ron. Brother Charlie was with her. They both waved up and she shouted, 'You be careful up there.'

I shouted back, 'Lovely day, Mrs Kray, for a spot of sunbathing!'

She smiled! I loved to see the twins on a visit with their mum. I'd be sitting on a visit chatting with my mum and dad, and feet away they would be there with Violet. I'd say to my mum, 'Nice to see, eh?'

I'd smile over at them – it was really nice times! Sure, it was prison but that visits room was always nice, relaxed and full of love. When the twins were in it, it was buzzing. They had this thing that just lit up a room; people could feel their presence!

After a visit, they were always smiling. Not like today – all most cons in prison seem to want is drugs, smuggled in up their rat's arses – and they're called men! This is today's villain – a new breed, or am I a dinosaur? Maybe it's time I went home!

Life on C Wing was crazy. One guy rammed a broom handle up his arse and got it stuck. They put him on a stretcher on his belly and carted him off to the hospital! He must have been pumping his arse with it! Kinky, what a sicko, he never did come back – too embarrassed.

I said, 'Maybe he did it so he could sweep the floor twice as quick.' Ron laughed at that – he loved a laugh.

There was always something mad going on at C Wing. Big George Wilkinson and Taffy Beecham took a screw hostage; a con got stabbed up. Dougie killed Brian Peak. Colin Robinson swallowing his razor blades and bedsprings; it was a fucking madhouse!

One day, John O'Rourke tapped Reg on the back. O'Rourke was a South Londoner, a big guy, bald head, liked to put it about that he was somebody special. Reg was leaning on the hot plate waiting for the lunch and when he felt that tap he spun round and let a right hook fly. O'Rourke was out cold! What a move, what a punch – it was awesome!

I loved that, we all did, and even Ron said it was the best punch ever! Marciano would have been proud of that one! But it never goes away in jail – the cunt was still around. He upset me next. So, I cut him up with a sauce bottle (badly). That was the end of C Wing for me, time to move on!

My memories with the twins on that wing are precious to me. That would be the last time I'd ever see them again on C Wing, but we would meet again – I knew it. Something told me our friendship had just begun. Ron and Reg would become family – if the truth be known, they loved me as the son they never had. I once told them that if it were possible I'd serve thirty years for them, just to see them walk free! And they knew I meant it.

* * * * *

I spent a lot of time in my prison life being moved from one dungeon to the next – from as far up as Durham to down in Wandsworth. A trail of destruction behind me; attacking screws, smashing up cells, you name it, I did it! But, all through those years, the twins stayed loyal; they sent me letters, cards, money and they even sent my mum and dad Christmas cards!

The grapevine in prison is as good as the Royal Mail, so I also got messages through it! On my travels, I heard a lot of shit spoken of the twins; the arguments I got into over them were amazing! They done this, they done that; they're this, they're that. Most of it was shouted through windows, as I could not do a lot about it! But the few odd times I could and did!

Once in Wandsworth, they put me out in the yard with some South London guy who was doing ten years for a blag. We were both doing punishment, and in them days you were not allowed to speak on exercise if you were on punishment. His name was Thompson and he had a massive beard. Anyway, we started talking, and a screw ordered us to shut up, so I spat in his face and carried on talking!

Thompson said, 'Blimey, you'll be in trouble for that.'

I said, 'Fuck it.'

As we walked around and passed the screw again, I spat on him again!

I shouted, 'Every time I pass you, I'll gob on you!'

The other screws were all tensed up ready for trouble; I was surprised they hadn't rung the bell. On the third time round, the screw had moved ... sensible, but I knew I was nicked! So I never gave a fuck!

Thompson said, 'Where are you from?'

I told him! We then got on to Parkhurst, and he said, 'Is that lunatic Ron Kray still there?'

I stopped. 'WHAT!'

He said it again, so I hit him! The bell went! By the time the screws got to me, I had smashed the granny out of him! The screws give it to me, but it was more for the spitting than for him! Such is life.

Another time I was in Walton Jail, Liverpool, and a Scouser bad-mouthed both Ron and Reg. I pulled him. 'Oi, you, what's your problem?'

He said, 'They're cunts!'

'Why?' I asked. 'Do you know them? Have you met them? Who are you? What are you?'

He got very aggressive and abusive. 'You're all the fuckin' same, you Londoners!'

The guy had a problem and it needed treatment; and he got it. I won't say any more on that, as I never got nicked for it, but he resembled a tea bag by the time I had finished with him!

In 1978, I returned to Parkhurst, back on C Wing! But it had all changed for the worse! Ron and Reg were no longer there – they had moved over to F Wing in the hospital! The truth is, they were sick of the cons on C Wing! The nutters, all the sieges, all the violence, it got too much. There was no peace on there, it was always on alert! C Wing would never be the same again.

My old pal Colin Robinson was still there, but even he was fed up. Even the screws started to get flash – there was no respect! Screws were starting to make themselves busy, which caused confrontations. I would go to the gym, but my heart wasn't in it. I actually missed Reg to work out with – I got a bit depressed, a black cloud covered me. I went through a very silent patch.

I asked the governor if I could go over to the hospital wing to see the twins. It was allowed, and they took me over to see them while they were on exercise. We had a walk in the yard for an hour and I felt a lot better. It was great to see them. They seemed happy over there.

But I was not happy on C Wing – it was a hellhole! Nobby Clarke arrived from Broadmoor and came on to C Wing. At this time, 1978, Nobby was without a doubt the most dangerous man in the system. He had a long grey beard, he was serving life and he had just been acquitted of a murder in Broadmoor! (Many still say he did it.)

Nobby just smiled. He was in his late forties to early

fifties and he knew he was never to be freed! He went to Broadmoor from Parkhurst in 1969 after the Parkhurst riot! Nobby made a spear and stabbed a Greek guy in the back! Was Nobby mad? I'd say he was ... different.

I've never met anybody like him since. He was very strange. He did weird things, such as tuning his radio into foreign stations, even though he could not speak any foreign languages. He pasted his cell walls with silver foil off tobacco packets, so it looked shiny. He saved up bags of dog ends – I mean big bags! His cell stunk of bacca; his fingernails were like talons – lethal! And he worshipped the devil! Nobby was, without a doubt, a very strange man. But I really liked him and I often had a mug of tea with him.

Then there was Ronnie Abrahams (the Screaming Skull – see my book *Legends*), all seven stone of him! Ron was in his forties, shaven headed and into yoga. He got life – in fact, he was sentenced to hang but he got reprieved two days before the execution. Now, I loved this guy. Mad, yes, but a hell of a character.

He would wrap his legs around his neck and do things to his body that the rubber man couldn't do; he was so supple and fit. He was a very quiet man, spoke little, but knew a lot. Occasionally, he would have an outburst, start shouting, throw things and even attack someone! But the Screaming Skull was a legend! He actually survived right up until 1999 and died in his cell at Frankland! He had served well over forty years. Incidentally, Nobby died in his cell in

1982; both these guys were legends; still remembered and always will be.

Once a week I was allowed over to the hospital to see the twins; it was the highlight of my week. I used to take them a parcel of tobacco, as they smoked a lot in those days, and I got some Typhoo tea bags for Ron, as he loved a strong cup of tea. He often said, 'You can't beat a fag and a cup of tea.'

Some of the lads were growing garlic at the time. The twins swore by it – good for the blood they said, and they ate a clove a day (raw). Reg loved a spoon of honey and Ron loved marmalade on toast; so I tried to get that as well.

The lads all put in a few bob, and I made sure I got what I could with it. But the twins were proud men; they used to give me a £20 note to help out! I'd see the tobacco baron and get it changed into half ounces of bacca. In those days, the currency was bacca; today it's drugs.

So I did what I could for the twins and I did my best. Some weeks were better than others. But nothing lasts in jail (not with me, anyway). C Wing was depressing me and violence finally erupted. Remember, I should have been on my way home. But, by this time, I had lost all my remission! I got more time added on. I was in a hole, and the hole was getting bigger. I cut up a con's face and slashed his body. I was charged with GBH with intent, my mind just went. Then, in the blackness, I attacked some screws!

This time I was put in a straightjacket and sent over to the hospital wing (I was kept in solitary), so I couldn't see anybody for ages! When I was seen by the police, I was put into a body belt (which is a restricting belt). I had to go to court; I was in trouble!

When I calmed down, Dr Cooper put me on F/2, which was the landing below the twins. We could talk through our windows. That cheered me up. They both gave me some good advice and sent me down some mags, papers and sweets.

When they used to go on exercise, most days, they would come to my door. It had a hatch in it for food to be passed through, so they could look in. I'd pass my hand out to shake theirs.

One day, Ron handed me a note and winked! I sat down and read it. It was the most touching letter I ever got. It said something like:

Please ... slow down! Don't end up like me.
Life is too precious to throw away,
You're young, full of life
Think of your mum when you feel bad
I don't want to see you like this
God Bless ... Ron

It sure made me think!

I was kept on my own; I even went out on the yard on my own. One day, Reg was escorted in from the yard by a dozen screws! He'd chinned a con! Then, days later, Ron chinned the same con! Twice the con got it. I thought that was funny (I bet the con never, though). It turned out the con was a pest.

There was one con Ronnie hated in that hospital. He worked on the hot plate serving the food. Ron despised him that much that, when the prick was, say, serving custard or soup or whatever, Ron would refuse to accept it.

Reg pulled the con and told him it would be best if he stopped working on the hot plate, as Ron disliked him! But the prat never took the advice. The inevitable had to happen. (I blame the screws, as they knew the potential was there!) Bash! The con got a tray in his face. So much for a warning.

At this time Ron had a toy-boy running around for him. It was Peter Gatrell. Reg hated him, as did we all! We could see right through it – he was basking, using Ron's name to get gifts off him! Jewellery, PT kit, favours. The guy was a ponce! Long curly hair, wiggled his arse in his skin-tight shorts. He got Ron right at it, flicking his eyelashes like that – a cup of acid into his boat would have done the trick!

It was fucking sick to watch, but, like all mugs, he disappeared. When he got out, he forgot Ron!

Then the day came when I lost the plot with a Welsh screw; he was a slag – always pushing me, testing me! It was a Sunday. I remember that because it was cornflakes, and we only had cornflakes once a week in those days.

Also that day, I was to get a visit. So I was all excited, but this screw started and I just saw red. He was a loud, aggressive sort, but I could see right through him: it was a front! He was basically a bully! We had words, then I did it – I cut him. At first I thought I missed him, then his face opened up, and blood gushed out. He was in shock. Other screws grabbed me, and bells were going as they piled on top of me. I could see above on F/3 laundry the cons were looking down. (Two of them were Ron and Reg; they were gutted!)

I was covered in blood (the screw's blood, mine was to come!). They carted me off to the box, known as the 'silent room' and I got it big time! By the time they left, I was in a terrible state, and all I could see was my visitors' faces in my head.

I was gutted! But not sorry! Why should I be sorry, I don't regret none of it, he got some of his own. That's life in prison: madness!

Once you're in that box, you're alone. That's when the real madness begins, the silence, the isolation, the mind games! They can do whatever they wish, you have no rights! You'll forget what day it is, what month it is; your friends become cockroaches and spiders, they're the only company you get.

The Parkhurst box has a hatch, which you get fed through – the door doesn't open. And the games start up: your food is cold, or spat on, your bread is stale, there's a bad smell about it. There's scouring powder in your tea. You damaged one of them and they don't like it; he's their friend, so they make it hard for you! You get abuse, even at night; you will get the light flicked on and off, and kicks on your door, all to antagonise you.

Life becomes a black hole of despair; you get very sick in the mind, and you're on the edge. You don't see any papers or books, there's a concrete shit hole that they pull the chain from outside to flush – you don't even get to control the launching of your own shit! Days will go by before they flush it. Flies come in, those little gnats that make so much noise in the night, you begin to feel great despair, you become on the edge, you're hated!

You start to hate yourself! You're insane, driven insane! There's no mirror, so I used to study my reflection in the concrete bowl, in the pool of water I'd look at my shadow on the wall; I'd walk up and down in a state of despair! I felt and I looked like shit!

No pen to write with, no radio, no news; silence eats into you. A straw mattress on the floor, one fireproof blanket, no pillow, no sheets, and no photos (all your mail is kept in a bag); you're in a concrete coffin, and you're dead. The screw will be on sick leave – full pay! He will get some compensation. I will get nine years added. He is laughing all the way to the bank. The system has won.

When I came out of that box, months later, I believe I left part of me in it; I was never the same again. I was charged again with GBH with intent, so now I had to face two trials. I got so down I went on to tranquillisers to switch off from it all.

It was also the time Ronnie Kray started to lose the plot. He attacked a governor and did a spell in the box! Later, he attacked a screw and he went back in the box again. Then I did too – we were in and out like yo-yos. I started to laugh a lot and could not control it; I would go into fits of laughter and start crying at the same time, and I laughed that much it hurt my ribs. I was having convulsions! Hysteria! But I never knew why I was laughing – it was fucking madness!

On another occasion, I jumped on a screw. The other screws all jumped on me and I was laughing all the way to the box as they bashed me! Yeah, laughing all the way to the strong box as they punched and kicked me. This time I freaked them out.

My court case began; it was 8 December 1978 (my granddad's birthday). I was certified insane and sectioned off to a max asylum for an indefinite period. Section 60/65. 'Indefinite' is unlimited. In fact, I was 'lifed off'. I could not be released until the asylum doctors (and the Home Secretary) agreed I was not a danger to the public.

The judge told me in no uncertain terms that I was a very dangerous man and that society had to be protected from me! I was taken back to Parkhurst in a state of shock. Dr Cooper awaited me. He told me I would be moving before Christmas to Rampton Asylum. My life was now to be spent in a madhouse.

From a seven-year prison sentence to a life in a madhouse to me was a fucking nightmare. My next couple of weeks were like a slow-moving dream. The lads all helped me through it. Especially Johnny Keibner – he stopped me smashing in a guy's head with a lump of brick – I just wanted to cave his head in. Why, I don't know. I just felt like it! Why not? What had I to lose?

Another day, I nutted out all the windows in the toilet in the yard. Blood was running into my eyes. It was Reggie Kray who got to me first, he held a T-shirt to my cuts! I don't know why I did it – it was madness! A couple of days before I left for Rampton, I slung a pot of shit over a screw – why? Why not! Yeah, why not!

The day came, 20 December 1978. Eight screws came for me. I was walked off F Wing, cuffed up and so confused. I walked up to F/3, and there they were, my two pals, Ron and Reg. 'Good luck,' they shouted!

Colin Robinson and Johnny Keibner were both locked behind their doors, but they shouted too. I was on my way to a new era, a new chapter to my life: fucking madness!

I did not want to go. I'd sooner have lived in the box! But I knew one thing: it was not the end of my relationship with the twins, I just knew it! Somehow, somewhere, our paths would cross again, I just knew it! Don't ask me how … it's intuition!

I was on my way to Rampton; across the ferry and along the road, it was a long journey to Nottinghamshire. We pulled into Oxford Jail, which was, I believe, one of the oldest jails in the UK (it's now closed down). We stopped for lunch. Only seconds after arriving there, I nutted a screw. I would have done a lot more but I was cuffed up to eight screws. This cocky cunt had got funny! He actually said, 'Shall we feed the loony!'

Well, I can say now, we never overstayed our welcome. Even the escort laughed about it! I couldn't get nicked, could I, as I was now officially 'insane'. Right at that moment I could have shot the Queen and not faced a trial, so it had its advantages!

As we drove on, I closed my eyes. I thought about the time at Parkhurst when I once went to Ronnie Kray's cell door in the hospital wing. It was at a time when Ron was himself was going through a bad spell. I looked in and saw him just sitting down staring into space, deep in thought!

Ron turned to look at me; it was a face of stone. His eyes were glazed over – it wasn't the Ron I knew.

'You OK, Ron?' I asked.

He got up and walked towards me slowly.

'You OK, Ron?' I repeated.

He said, 'I'm fucking sick of this place, sick of it.'

I passed my hand through his hatch and touched his shoulder. 'Keep it together, Ron, keep it strong,' I said.

I never forgot that: me, of all people, telling him to keep it together! But I meant it from the heart. I felt a lot for Ron, he was special.

Until I landed in this place, I really was wet behind the ears as to what madness was all about. Rampton was the pits of insanity. This gaff was king of the loony bins! And, believe me, it was hard work for me! (It's all in my autobiography, remember; this is the Krays' story, not mine!)

So, as I lived my life in the asylum, the twins were still with me. Violet Kray sent me a nice tracksuit and some trainers with a nice card telling me to behave! Reg sent me some photos, all signed to me, with a sad letter saying Ron had gone into a bad state of depression and was on a lot of medication. He was in fact in the box, isolated after having attacked two screws!

Colin Robinson had swallowed another bedspring (you may well ask how the fuck anybody could swallow a bedspring, but he does it easily). Parkhurst seemed the same. But I was now no part of jail – I was a professional lunatic! Slash Walters was there – now, he had been a good pal of the twins in the Fifties and Sixties. Ron used to tell me all about him – he cut up more people than Sweeney Todd.

Over the weeks and months that followed, there was a lot written about the twins. (Would they survive now they were apart? Would Reg go mad? Could Ron get better? What would happen now?)

Violet had to travel to the Isle of Wight and Crowthorne village in Berkshire to see her two sons – that lady never missed a visit to each of the twins every week! Imagine it: add up the thousands of miles she had to travel each year to see her boys, and Charlie when he was serving his sentence; that's some loyalty for a

mother. She was one special mum, a true diamond.
Everybody loved that special lady.

The twins' real friends stayed loyal, men like Joe
Pyle, Roy Shaw, Jack Lee, Wilf Pine, Alec Steine,
Freddie Foreman ... all men of steel, men of honour,
not like the fucking men of today.

* * * * *

My life plodded on. Rampton just grew on me; I learned
to handle the madness best by being mad. They had me
on injections and I spent long periods in isolation. They
did a lot of evil things to me there, even whipped me
with wet towels! But that's life; I survived.

It made my day, week and year when I got a letter
from Ronnie! (My first for a good eight months.) Reggie
wrote regularly, but Ron's letters really lifted me up! He
seemed to be well and settling into Broadmoor. (Oh, I
should add now that the twins' writing was identical and
very difficult to read, though with time it became easy.)

Ron said the visits were good and that alone had
cheered him up. As in Broadmoor, it's not like prison:
you can have a visit every day, see who you want. As
we are all Cat A, our visitors have to be checked and
passed by the police.

So, Reg was on two visits a month; Ron could have
two a day if he wanted! And he made up for the lost
years – he had more visits in a month than he had had
in ten years in jail!

A lot of people went up to see Ronnie – Diana Dors, Alan Lake, Debbie Harry, Richard Harris, the Kemp brothers, boxers, film stars, singers, dancers, comedians. They're all his friends, he made up for lost time all right, and good luck to him; everyone was happy for him. He wore his made-to-measure suits, his crocodile shoes, his best aftershave; he even ordered salmon sandwiches and non-alcoholic lagers. He smoked his civvy fags and became the Lord of Broadmoor.

* * * * *

After ten long hard and weary months in Rampton (I mean fucking hard), I had absorbed it all! Beatings! Drugs! Abuse! Isolation! It had a serious effect on my mind; I was not the same guy! I was called into the office one day, surrounded by screws; my doctor, Dr Perrera, was sitting at the desk.

'Well, I've got some news for you! You're moving, we can no longer do anything for you! You're too dangerous to keep here, so you're moving to Broadmoor!'

I felt like I had won the lottery, I was elated! I was going to be with Ron again! Who said miracles don't happen?

Rampton, for me, was a disgrace. A fucking joke! We were supposed to be sent there to be helped. Anyway, read my autobiography, it will tell you what a hellhole it is. Fuck it, I was off! Broadmoor Costa Del Sol here I come! Yippee, get the salmon out; I'm on my way!

Although I was on my way to Broadmoor to be with Ron, I had previously spent time in the notorious Ashworth Asylum. At this time, the place was actually called Park Lane Special Hospital; it changed its name to Ashworth in 1986. It must be the most modern max-secure asylum in Europe; it was like leaving hell and entering paradise!

I was put on to Hazlett Ward and, from day one, I felt like a human. My room was like a flat: TV, bed, locker, toilet, sink and even a carpet! The food was brilliant; the facilities were brilliant, a gym, a pool, snooker, library and canteen, and good money! Everything was just great but, like all madhouses, it had its problems: in a word, madness! As you'd expect, being full of insane people, the place was insane! And I must say now, never in my life have I seen so much homosexuality. Ronnie would have loved it there, it was alive with gays!

There was one who dressed like a woman, even down to the handbag and make-up! Thank fuck he/she or 'it' wasn't on my ward, but I saw 'it' walking around the grounds; even the wiggle was real!

I once saw 'it' walking hand in hand with another nutcase, but this nutcase thought he was Elvis: quiff, sideburns the lot. I was in a fucking circus!

There was all sorts of clowns here. Some dangerous ones, too! John Henry Gallagher, now John Morrison. I cut him up in his cell at Hull Jail in 1975, evil bastard. He was doing seven years for mugging a vicar! Then he got out and killed four old people! Yeah, four.

Still, he won't ever get out again, so don't worry. If I had blinded the rat in 1975, four people would not have been murdered; fate is strange. But it was nice to see his ugly scars!

I didn't last long. They alleged that I tried to drown a big fat paedophile in the pool. He was saved and I was banned from using the pool. I'll say no more, but accidents do happen! The slag should not have been in the pool.

Little Joe Warren was there, an old pal of the twins. Stevie Booth was also there – he'd moved there from Rampton. You just can't get away from the legends. I had some good pals there (some of old): Chris Reed, Ron Greedy, Steve Roughton, Lenny Doyle, some good old lads.

Visits were brilliant too, so I got myself some nice ones and basically got on with my life. By this time, I had served eleven years. Yeah, eleven fucking years; considering my original sentence was only seven years, and I should have only served four years and eight months, eleven years is a bit crazy. But that's how mad life can end up. I was serving a longer sentence than a lot of killers serve, and I was still in max secure, still considered a danger to the public!

I had all my special photos up in frames in my Ashworth flat: my family on one wall, my friends on another wall. I had lots of photos of the Krays, all signed to me.

One day I noticed one of the photos was missing, a

framed photo of Ron and Reg taken with Rocky Marciano and George Raft! Nicked! But by who? I had a think and put it down to one of three people. It was only guesswork, and I could have been wrong (if I was wrong then so be it), but I had to try and find out! So I made a plan.

I called number one in my room! As he walked in, I smashed him in the face, then held him up. I got a pencil and held it just inside his ear! 'Right, where's my photo? Three seconds and I ram this pencil into your brain. One, two ...'

'No, no! It's in my cupboard, I'll get it for you.'

See, kindness is rewarded.

CHAPTER 4

THE MADNESS OF RONNIE KRAY... AND ME

Madness. I'll tell you what madness is.

Madness is pain and more pain.

Ronnie was mad – that man suffered! 'Mental illness' is a terrible torture. You can turn on anybody at any time! But my madness was never 'mental'; mine was unpredictable.

There is no diagnosis; you can't diagnose it when it's not known. But I've been there, many times. So many times that I feel I'm on an elastic band – it's now a part of my character.

Lying naked in a square concrete box, all wrapped up like a Christmas turkey. Ankle straps, body belt – and I'm not talking kinky Jamie Theakston stuff here – this is what madness is ... pain, not pleasure!

You wanna piss, so you roll over and do it on the floor! You look at your reflection in the piss and see your face all busted up, bruised and swollen; you feel the tears (hot) well up in your eyes, not in sadness but in frustration, pain! You just want to hurt somebody for the humiliation, you never forget it, you can't!

Hours pass you by, your arms go numb. Cramp ... more pain, you feel sick, mentally you're on the edge – in fact, there is no edge, you've fallen! You're in a black hole. It's a bottomless abyss, there is no light, hope has been sucked away!

You're nonexistent; you're a dead man breathing. But even the breathing is painful. Once I recall lying there in this box, watching a spider up in the corner of the ceiling. I'm sure that spider was laughing at me, it seemed to be waving a leg at me, as if to say, 'Hey, you look funny.'

I thought, When I'm let out of this contraption, I'll kill you! No spider mugs me off like that!

Another piss time is staring at the stains on the wall: food stains, tea stains and blood stains! Have you ever looked at that 'always' mysterious shaped pattern that the newspapers throw at us from time to time when they haven't any news to fill their pages? The sort of shape that you have to stare at for so long, then look away and you can see the face of what is thought to be Jesus Christ. Well, if you look hard enough at the stains on the walls and for long enough, you'll see a face, a picture. Then you blink and it moves. It may even talk to you. In your madness it will help you through.

Then a dozen guards will come in, to see how you

are, or to see if you want some more 'treatment' ('Can you take more?'). It's your choice: get lemon with them and you'll have it, they don't mess about, nor are they shy about giving you second helpings. Yeah, madness comes in all sorts of life. But it all ends up painful.

Ronnie would sometimes bang up, for a day or two, to try to sort it out. But silence, loneliness, only eats you away; it breeds more madness.

I remember the day Reg cut his wrists, when he was in Long Lartin Jail – and I mean cut! He almost bled to death! That place made Reg mad! So they moved him back to Parkhurst! It was really not like Reg to do that, it was against his character, but madness can affect anybody at any time!

Why did Michael Ryan shoot up Hungerford? Or that prat who shot John Lennon? Why did Jeffery Palmer eat all his victims? What made the Ripper rip up? Madness!

You go to bed a normal guy and you wake up a lunatic. It's a fact. Hey, even Adolf Hitler's mother loved him – she said he was a lovely baby. Madmen are not born with horns, but madness is in the blood, and it comes out if you wait long enough.

Poor old Ron suffered most of his life; he never really found any peace of mind.

Sure, we've got feelings and emotions, but sadly some people have to be served up, some only learn by a crash!

I think age, and the maturity that generally comes

CHARLES BRONSON

with it, can cure a lot of madness. But, when you're real old, you go mad again with senility, so you can't escape madness! It comes to us all, so I say enjoy it, kick some ass, and keep on kicking until the angels come!

So what's the difference between Rampton and Broadmoor? I'll tell you. Broadmoor has a different sort of lunatic. A better quality of madness – the elite! The cream! The guv'nors! Let me explain something that only I can explain: Rampton is for (no disrespect) the silly mad people! I don't want to be nasty, but they're a bit simple, not big brains.

Broadmoor is more for the 'Mad Professors' – high IQs, dangerous minds! Get the picture? You want proof? Look it up: Rampton was built in 1908 for the mentally subnormal. Obviously we have come a long way since then, but it still has that stigma and it still caters for the silly loons!

Broadmoor, on the other hand, was built for the criminally insane: men and women who are a serious threat to the state. The first nutcase there was a guy who tried to murder the royal family. I believe that was in the 1890s and since then it has taken the elite of the insane: Donald Hume, Ian Ball, Roy Shaw, Frank Mitchell, Marty Frape, Timmy Noonan, George Heath, Ron Kray and of course, yours truly!

Madness is a gift of life, as Ronnie once said, but you need to be in control of it; lose control and you lose your soul – lose your soul and you're a dead man dreaming.

So I arrived at the most famous asylum on the

76

planet! Or should that be 'infamous'? Like Alcatraz; Colditz; Spandau; Devil's Island; Sing Sing; St Quentin. But Broadmoor is the elite of all these establishments, the number one: you can't compare it to any other institution on this planet. The superintendent at Broadmoor at this time, in the 1970s, said to me, 'We only take the best here.' I didn't know whether it was a compliment, or an insult (but I later broke his heart – he hated me. I'll come to why later). Yes, I'd made it! I was in the big house! As the van drove in and the gates slammed shut, I felt ready for a new challenge! I was put on to Somerset Ward, which was the admission ward, this is where my home would be for the next few months, and where they would assess me and monitor me.

Doctors, shrinks, psychologists, all sorts of idiots, prying into my life, drilling into my brain with their words to see how I tick. Fucking idiots! They can't even sort their own lives out, let alone mine! Most of them are divorced or gays, but they want to rule my life! I don't think so. Only a fool would open up to this lot. Us loons in Broadmoor are not fools, we are the elite, we tell them only what they want to hear, not our secrets. It's a game, like chess: they move and we move. That's all it is and all it ever will be! Keep off my toes and I'll keep off yours; fuck with me, you fuck with hell. Simple as that.

So there I am in Somerset Ward, Broadmoor. They let me have a bath, they fed me and gave me the rules. One said, 'We tame tigers here.' Oh, yeah, well, I'm a lion, so fuck off. It's all psychological, see, testing the water. What can they do to me? Only one thing that I haven't already had, death. So what's new? We all gotta die anyway, and I told them just that: 'Kill me or drop me out!'

It was the next day that they let me into the day room with all the other loonies. I walked into a room with 25 madmen (25 including me, that is). They were all sat in soft chairs with crazy expressions, bulging eyes and drugged up. Then I saw two lovely faces: Ron Kray and Colin Robinson. It was like heaven! I was amazed to see them. I knew Colin had been nutted off, and I knew Ron was here, but I did not expect to be on the same ward as them, let alone to see them.

Ron came up and shook my hand and we hugged. He looked ill; he'd lost a lot of weight, he had aged and looked drawn. That hellhole box in Parkhurst had taken a lot out of him; I knew the misery it held.

'Ron,' I said, 'great … it's magic to see you.'

I then hugged Colin; he also looked a bit sick, as he'd just had another op to cut another bedspring out.

Ron took me over to his locker and opened it. It was full of tins of food and bars of chocolate. He piled a load into my locker – salmon, fruit, chocs, the lot. Then we had a cup of tea and a chat.

He told me all about what the slags had put him through at Parkhurst. It was sad to hear it all, but now he was on the proper medication and he was getting back to some quality of life.

'It's not so bad,' he told me. 'The food is good, but the

hard part is all the loons.' He warned me to be on my toes. The sad bit was that he and Colin were to be moved on to new wards, as their assessment was over; mine had just begun!

Ron's visits were on the ward in a room, as would mine be (us ex-prisoners were treated differently). It was all security for us: screws sat in the room to listen to us and see how we were with our visitors.

From the day room, I saw Violet and Charlie Kray come in. I waved and shouted to them and they waved back. Ron later told me that they said I looked fit and well, they wished me luck and said to behave!

Broadmoor was not like jail. Visitors could bring up gifts, food and clothes and the like. This is when Violet started to leave me a box of goodies every time she visited Ron. And if she didn't turn up, Charlie did. It was the start to my famous apple pies; there would always be some apple pies in the box, some sweets and a cake! Charlie used to leave mags and books and the East London papers! I respected it. But those apple pies, I used to love. I now have a strong passion for pies. I once took a hostage for some apple pies – that's what you call a real passion!

Ron, Colin and me used to sit together, chat and have a laugh, but at times, Ron would sit alone and think a lot – deep thoughts. Also, there was a loony on the ward Ron fancied. He was about 23 years old, slim and good-looking; I don't think he even needed to shave! Sometimes Ron would vanish into the recess with him for ten minutes and always used to come out with a smile. I suppose, for Ron, it was a lot easier being gay, as he could still be loved; for us straight guys we had no love, it's frustrating, and it's tension. Over the years, it's insanity. Men need sex, even dogs do, it's a release – and it's why we resort to violence, as we need some loving!

Which reminds me, once in Parkhurst Prison hospital wing, I walked into the recess room and Ron was in there alone just looking out of the window up into the sky; there was a breeze coming in through the window. He was silent, just staring out!

'You OK, Ron?'

'Yeah, just looking out, it's a lovely night.'

That's how Ron was – deep. He loved nature.

One day, Ron and me were sitting chatting when a loon came over and got very personal. He almost demanded some fags off Ron! Ron had packets of them and he gave most away; nobody went short of a smoke when Ron was close by. He looked after people. But he hated greedy bastards. Ron's face turned white, his whole face changed into a mask of hate; I grabbed his arm. 'Leave it to me, Ron, please.'

I pulled Colin and asked him to watch my back; I had to be careful, as eyes were all over! I managed to grab this demanding loon's windpipe and push him into the recess. I then smashed his head into the wall a dozen times, then washed the blood off my hands. I came back out happy.

About ten minutes later, they found him. We all had banged up in our cells! I was questioned and so was Colin, but nothing came of it; the loon went to the hospital wing, but he never came back! Such is life in the asylum! I played a lot of chess; I do love a game of chess. One loony was a grand master! He flipped outside and killed a fella with an axe ('cos he beat him). I told you, unique people, the best of madness. Oh I did beat him once, so that makes me a grand master too, but I did nick his bishop. (Well, you've got to sometimes to win.)

I'd only been at Broadmoor a short while and I was sitting there next to Ronnie when this geezer comes in and sits down. He keeps staring at me.

I tell him, 'Listen, mate, if you don't stop staring at me I'm going to punch your lights out!'

He says in a puffy voice, 'Can I have a word in private with you?'

'Not now, I'm watching the telly,' I said.

'Look, I'll meet you down the recess in five minutes,' he says.

So I thought, Aye, aye, we've got a fucking shirt-lifter here.

Anyway, I went to the recess area and he was there. 'I want you to punch me,' he says.

'Look, I don't want to do that, you've done nothing to deserve a hiding,' was my reply.

But he insisted, so I gave him a right-hander, a real corker of a shot followed up by a left, a right upper cut and another left. He went down and hit his head off a urinal, out stone cold he was. So I dragged him over to a sink and slung some water on him. When he started to come around I could see he had a hard on in his pants and he'd shot his load and he was moaning in that puffy voice, 'Oh, oh, that was lovely.'

I've got nothing against puffs so long as they leave me alone.

Anyway, I goes back to watch the telly and I says to Ron, 'Do you know what that geezer wanted?'

Ron said, straight out, 'He wanted you to hit him. He looks for the newest people here and that's what turns him on.'

But there was a few times Ron stopped me from knocking a few of them out – he told me it wasn't worth it.

On Saturdays, we used to go down the sports field to watch the football. The Broadmoor team was mostly young lads (late teens, early twenties); sometimes outside teams used to come in and play. It was always a good fast game.

Ron loved it. It was funny really, he used to say, 'Oh, lovely ... look at the bum on No. 8,' and 'Look at the legs on No. 3 ... ooh, lovely!'

I'd say, 'I'm off for a walk, Ron.'

A lot of loons upset Ron pestering him: 'Can I have this?', 'Will you sign this?' or 'Got any fags?' Loons would not leave him alone! I pulled so many: 'Leave him alone.' But you can't reason with loons, they don't listen. I lost count of how many I chinned, but you can't chin the whole asylum. Poor old Ron got fed up of it and finally stopped going down the field.

* * * * *

On a scale of one to ten, how mad was Ronnie Kray? Ten. Make no mistake about it, ten! Another example. I'm going back now to Broadmoor, Somerset Ward One in 1979; I had my best time with Ron around then. That place holds some fucking good memories. Ron's cell was about five away from mine. He had a Brummie lunatic next door to him; we hated him – one mad loon he was. He used to break wind on purpose, to wind people up.

One day Ron said, 'Enough is enough!'

I said, 'What's up, Ron?'

He said, 'That Brummie prat farted near me in the recess when I was shaving, then he smiles!'

I said, 'I'll have a word with him and sort it.'

I pulled the Brummie in the day room – he used to sit by the window, forever looking out of the window he was.

'Oy! Brummie, what's your problem?'

'Eh?' he replied.

'All the farting, you farted near Ron.'

'Fuck Ron!' he said. 'I will fart where and when I want.'

Well, what can you say to that? He said it all. He had to have some.

Believe me, Brummie did not fart again anywhere near Ron. In fact, the last I seen of him, he was being carried out to the infirmary – he had a big hole in the back of his head. Strange people, strange place.

I have watched Ron smoke ten fags, one after the other, then stop, have a cuppa and a cough and then back on a fag. A lot of his fags he only smoked half of before stubbing them out.

A lot of loonies lived off Ron's ashtray – they never had to buy fags, they had plenty with Ron's stubs. Somerset Ward Two was not a great place, as we were only being assessed, monitored to see what we would be allocated to, so it was just the basics.

We couldn't even have a radio in our cells, but I never would have in Broadmoor because there is always somebody singing some shit. You have a lot of Christmas carols and hymns at night off the religious nutters.

After a while, you just sing along with them. Some nights, there would be a dozen or more loons singing 'Onward Christian Soldiers' or some shit like that, and it echoes in old places like Broadmoor. I have even heard the night watchman joining in as he does his checks.

Ron used to look at me in the morning and say, 'Did you fucking hear that lot last night? It is a fucking madhouse.'

I said, 'Yes, even the mad watchman was singing.'

I remember the time Ron almost strangled a loon; in fact, if it hadn't been for the screws, the loon would have been brown bread (dead). After that, Ron spent six months over in Norfolk Ward, underneath in the dungeon.

Eventually, when Ron left for Somerset Ward Three, where he could have his possessions, he had a pure china teapot sent in. Oh yes, he loved his cuppas. Well, so does everyone, but not thirty cups a day …

Ron wasn't much for games. He only played pool once in all the time I was with him – he just never had the patience for games. I only played it twice myself, and in one of those games I hit a guy with a cue – the loon was cheating.

Once a week on Somerset Ward One, we could have a meal brought in from the local curry house. (Obviously we had to pay; well, it is a hospital, and not a prison. We were patients, not prisoners.) Just because it has got a thirty-foot wall, so what! One week, Ron ordered thirty-odd meals. That's how he was, generous to a fault. He bought everyone a meal; I ended up with six of them, as some of the loons didn't like curry. What a feast that was.

There was the mad occupational therapy shit we used to go to. Fuck knows why, because all we did was sit there and chat or play cards, but on reports it looks good. Ron used to sit there, drink tea and chat.

Ron was the best-dressed madman in Britain. Nobody in Broadmoor dressed like him: he had loons polishing his shoes, ironing his shirts, making his bed and watering his plants.

Ron was the original Lord of the Manor. His then

wife, Kate, used to bring him up some lovely clothes, shirts, ties and all sorts. Ron loved a silly tie; he would think fuck all of paying £200 for a tie or a grand for his crocodile shoes.

Did Ron have a drink there? Well, what do you think? Don't you think he had it all summed up? Ask Kate. She was forever giving those white coats backhanders. Well, they are human, aren't they? Wouldn't you sell a bottle of vodka for fifty quid? The time arrived when Ron and Colin moved wards and I was left alone, with a room full of people I never got on too well with. It was now all uphill for me. Ron went to Somerset Ward Three, Colin went to Cornwall Ward, and I stayed on Somerset Ward One.

Then, George Shipley arrived from Feltham Borstal. He livened the day room up and it cheered me up big time! One day, I went into the recess bursting for a slash and I caught a loony right up another loon's arse, pumping away, he was like a piston. While I was peeing, I could hear it. I felt sick, it just got too much for me and I attacked them both! What made me sick was that they were both old codgers in their fifties and one was a paedophile! That done it for me, a man can only stand so much, what was I supposed to do! Accept it, ignore it?

Then another time, a loon actually shit himself in the day room. Why? Not a clue! But he did it, it stank and he thought it was funny, he shook his legs and it fell out all over the floor, all over his shoes! Fucking get me out of here... I'm going mad!

Another time, one loon stabbed another in the eye with a pen! One would nut walls; one would laugh so much he had to be injected! George and me, we tried to carry on regardless. But it was almost impossible not to let it get to you. Yes, it was hard.

My mum and dad visited me regularly. When I told them about some of the loons, they laughed, but a lot of these loons were lethal! Killers of the worst degree. One killed his wife and four kids with a hammer – five innocent people! He was a white-collar worker, never been in trouble in his whole life, he just went berserk. Why? Who knows!

Barry Williams was there – he shot four people dead for no reason!

Ian Ball was there. He almost kidnapped Princess Anne!

Donald Hume was there. He murdered Stanley Setty, a used-car dealer from the East End of London, cut up his body and threw his dismembered body parts from a plane into the Essex Marshes. The murder marked the first recorded murder using an airplane. If Hume had not mistaken the water-covered marshes for open sea the body of Setty may never have been found. He threw Setty out of the plane over the Channel!

Yeah, some right legendary characters, but believe it there was some right monsters in there too. Child killers, mass rapists, fuck me; I even met the wolf man. I even bumped into Adolf Hitler – all in black, a tash, he marched up and down the corridors. He said he was Adolf and he believed it. I met them all: Jesus, the Pope,

Jimi Hendrix! I met one loony who believed he was Mad Frank Fraser! Yeah, Frank Fraser, this guy idolised him so much he believed he was him! We are talking the maddest bastards on the planet! Twenty-four-carat loonies – now see what I mean!

After four months on Somerset One, it was my time to move on. They put me on Gloucester Ward. From day one, I hated it, hated it! And I knew it would be a disaster! I told them, 'Put me on Ron's ward', but they said he was settled and they didn't want me to unsettle him. So that was it: off to Gloucester Ward I went!

I lasted only days. In that time I lost the plot. I just felt mad; I was at the most dangerous I had ever been! The problems I had were magnified by the madness around me! The ward had the maddest fuckers you could wish to meet! One loon invited me into his room and showed me a spider in a box. 'Meet Billy,' he said. I looked at him, then the spider, it was no bigger than a smartie (in fact, it looked lifeless). It was probably dead.

'Go on … stroke it, stroke Billy,' he said.

Was this cunt real? He never had a smile, he was real all right.

'Billy's my pal,' he told me.

'Oh, yeah, what's his game then?' I asked

'He's a killer, poisonous; I set him on people!'

'Oh, yeah … look, mate, do me a favour!'

As I went to leave he did something that told me I was in a place I didn't want to be – he shouted, 'Get him, Billy. Attack!'

I stopped and looked at him. He was serious. I felt sad and depressed.

'Get him, Billy!'

I walked out defeated. That done me! How could I hit him, what could I do? Days later, I was moved over to Norfolk intensive care unit, which was the hellhole of Broadmoor. The punishment ward. Isolation. Special watch. Security. This would be my home for four-and-a-half years. I was now Broadmoor's most violent man and my life was to be total security! Until I landed in Norfolk Ward, I was wet behind the ears. Now my test was on. The test of survival!

So there was Ron, nice and settled, a TV in his room, nice food, great visits, a bit of comfort and a good quality of life. And I was in a stinking cell, a filthy piss pot, no air, no companionship, alone and empty and being driven mad!

They also had me on injections and pills. I spent most of my time asleep, in a cloud of despair. My dreams were nightmares, and my existence was a 'lifemare'!

I became desperate, dangerous and totally unpredictable. I tried to strangle somebody, I smashed things up, but all I got was bashed up and drugged! Every time I rebelled, I got it back big time! I had to fuck with the system. The time had arrived for my first roof job in Broadmoor. It was 1981; I would hit them where it hurt – in the pocket. So up I went ... King of the Castle.

This one cost a million pounds' damage! It was at this

time I was labelled the 'million dollar man' – some label! Well, footballers now go for £10 million, it's nothing today, but back in the early 1980s it was some price! Especially for a Broadmoor madman!

Still, it was worth it just to see Ron's face light up! It was ages since I'd seen him properly. It seemed that the only time I would ever see him was when I did a roof job on Broadmoor's ancient and sacred building! The joke was at that time, 'I only do it to see Ron.'

Reg was usually allowed to visit Ron, once every three months. A big escort of screws from Parkhurst used to bring him. Reg would be all shackled up and driven to the asylum. Ron used to lay on some grub, and they would have two hours together in a room with all the screws! Four times a year they would get to see each other! (Eight hours every 365 days!) Not a lot, is it? Work it out; it's really a disgrace, an insult to humanity.

Ron would always write to me days before Reg was due. He would be excited. You could sense it. It's no secret, they were psychic. Ron told me about it: if Reg was ill, or vice versa, they would sense it. Twins are really one soul – I believe that. When one dies, the other lives on in agony.

So after three days I end up back in a hole! Alone! Empty! Back to a lifemare! The doctors and screws said, 'Never again, that's the last time you ever do our roof, no more, enough is enough.' Slam!

Behind the door is a coffin. Silence becomes part of

your existence; I had no radio, no books, just my mind. My shadow was the only movement I could see; it's not a nice way to live! But it's still a life – you have to learn to accept it; I would sleep a lot, daydream; think; plot and plan.

Reggie's life was still Parkhurst; fuck knows how he managed it! Reg actually held the record for being the longest con ever in Parkhurst in one stay. Seventeen years in one jail – that's awesome!

Broadmoor's longest-serving con – er, patient – had forty-plus years' service (but that was an asylum). And you know what, they weren't even awarded a CDM (Cadbury's Dairy Milk) for their long service record!

Reg had his problems, the same as all of us. You can't be infamous and not expect problems. Young cons after a name! But, throughout his journey, I would say Reg handled it well; he helped more than he harmed.

Word got back that some rat had tried to do Reg in the shower. Why? For what reason, I don't know, but Reg was fast and laid him out! When Reg hit you, you was cold.

Prison is very unpredictable; at any moment it can go up, and Reg saw it all. He was even there for the 1969 riot! He saw killings; he saw things you would not believe! Like the time Johnny Paton stabbed to death a con in the dinner queue! The con fell down dead and cons were just stepping over him as if he wasn't there! This was John's second murder in jail. He later hanged himself, as he knew he was a dead man walking.

Johnny Paton was, in fact, from my home town of
Luton, and the crazy thing was, he was a nice guy. But
he just lost it at times!

Reg was there when the IRA got up on the roof and
pulled it off ... he was there when Billy Skingle, the cop
killer, escaped out of the SSU, only to be captured
within hours. He was there when Rocky was killed in
the kitchen; Reg had seen it all and more!

While Ron was living on salmon and smoking good-
quality fags, Reg was on porridge and in a battlefield.
Reg did have his work cut out, but strangely enough I
think he loved the challenge! He became a fitness
fanatic, packed in smoking and kept himself in good
shape. Rumours went around that Reg was like Ron,
queer! Well, let me tell you: he was no queerer than
Romeo was. Reg just enjoyed young company.

He did not like to be with other villains and gangsters
(he found it depressing talking about crime). He could
see no point in sitting in a cell full of villains talking
about crime; what they had done; what they intend to
do; it was all dreams to Reg! He mixed with young cons;
because it kept him alive and active; they kept him up
to date. He enjoyed their company and they enjoyed
his. OK, in later years, he succumbed to his basic
instincts and turned bi, but I blame the system for that,
not him. It's what kept him sane.

Reg was a positive man; he would make something
work out of nothing, a great biz man – full of ideas! He
was always scheming and planning for his next

venture; his first book was on cockney rhyming slang. The other books followed: poetry, philosophy, a biography, he was always creative. Reg became the true legend of Parkhurst – the tales he could tell!

That 'Norman Parker' wrote Parkhurst tales, but Reg should have done it, not Parker! Reg was the Tale! He was the Rudolph Hess, the Papillon, the Birdman of Parkhurst, all rolled into one! Reg was the man, the ultimate survivor; fuck knows how he never went mad ... or did he? Madness can come in different forms!

So the years at Broadmoor flew by. They said I'd never hit the roof again – how wrong they were!

My third time on the roof ... oh God ... I'm in heaven! He lifted me all the way up ... he held me there ... I kissed that sky again! Who said madness doesn't pay!

'Hi, Ron!' I shouted down to him. He couldn't believe it! If looks could tell a story ... it was heavenly!

It was around this time that Ron married a woman called Elaine Mildner. Crazy, really – it baffled me! She was a mother of two, a divorcée and a penfriend to Reg. She was no beauty, but I'd say she had a good heart and she was not in it for the limelight, as she was a shy sort. Even Reg thought it crazy! Oh well, Ron was Ron! But the fact was, everyone knew it could not work.

Steph King, a pen friend, was a great source of strength to Ron; she sorted a lot out for him. Her friendship was loyal and honest. Ron admired her, that's a fact. He trusted Steph with his life – so let it be known that Nottingham people breed good-quality women! Steph also helped me over some bad patches in later years; which I thank her for; you're never forgotten, Steph!

Well, as I've said before, nothing lasts! Broadmoor had five years out of my life. Four-and-a-half of those years were in Norfolk Ward – shit years! But it cost them dearly! It was time to leave! Broadmoor and me had our last confrontation, the day I left, they cheered – it was in the press – but the fact was, I won! I'd never see Ron again. But our friendship was not over – it was to get stronger with time!

They used to try to intimidate me, scare me, tell me I would be a forty-year patient; I'd die there, blah, blah! All the mind games, but I kept hold of my dignity; I spat on the place as I stepped in the van! That was 1984, but I left behind some sad memories.

The saddest was the death of Mrs Violet Kray. I believe that a part of the twins died with her when she went. She was a great source of strength to them. It was such a sad time. The media went mad, as usual. The day of her funeral was the first day out for the twins in fourteen years and the media had a field day! There they were in their suits, surrounded with all the security, they were both cuffed up to the biggest screws (so as to make them look small) – it's the system's way to mug you off! They're good at that; but the twins stood proud, strong and dignified.

Yes, it was a great loss for them; and Charlie took it

bad too. Soon after Violet passed away, their dad died, but this time they decided not to go to the funeral – as they never wanted another circus! They would show their respect in their own silent ways. Alone and deep thoughts!

It's the same old story: you don't know how much you love somebody till they die. When they die, it's too late to tell them. So all you youngsters with mums and dads, give 'em a hug; say you love them; stay out of jail … don't put them through this hell! 'Cos if you do, in time you'll end up very sad!

Oh, I almost forgot – the superintendent. It was when I went up on my second roof, in 1983, that he came to hate me. Why? Well, he was days away from retirement and I went up! He had to retire a very sad man. After all, how would you like to be the superintendent of the world's number-one asylum and then some fucking lunatic gets up on the roof chucking off slates and wrecking the place! It doesn't get you a golden handshake, does it? He actually came to the window, almost begged me to come down. I slung a slate at him and he left that window a very dejected man!

I left happy; sad to leave behind my old mate Ronnie, but he was big enough to handle it! And every day after that he looked up to the roof he would remember me! He would have seen me up there like it was yesterday; and so will all the other guys in that place, the screws, the docs, all of them! Even the people in Crowthorne village. Those kids shouting at me to jump are now grown-ups with kids of their own! Hell, they may be working in Broadmoor or even locked up in there; whatever, they won't forget me! Nor will I forget them – how can you forget a part of history?

And before I forget! There's all of those people out there bragging about how they knew the Krays, blah, blah. Well, the twins got me a pocket watch. That watch is the greatest gift I ever had; priceless. It's also inscribed to me – yeah, to me! I told you all … they loved me! See the photo section in this book for the proof!

So when is the movie being done on the Krays' life inside? Now that would be some movie! A true winner! Their life inside was as colourful as it was outside! I remember once in Parkhurst, in 1976, the twins were telling me about Jonathan Silver, the biggest guy they'd ever seen. Now this guy was fucking awesome! (I would later meet him myself.) Anyway, Jonathan Silver was 6ft 11in tall with a size fifteen shoe! He weighed twenty-plus stone; he was an ex-Coldstream guardsman, so with his furry hat on his head he was nine fucking feet tall!

Anyway, something flipped in his nut! One day he lost the plot, he killed his three kids and almost his wife and himself. He ended up in Brixton the same time as the Krays' Firm!

Now he may have been a giant, but he was also a child killer, so he got scalded, attacked, all sorts; broken glass was put into his porridge, buckets of shit were slung in his cell. Someone attempted to burn him alive; eventually he was isolated from the other cons. He was sent for trial, found to be 'insane' and sent to Broadmoor!

It was 1979 when I bumped into him. (If you read one of my many other books, *Silent Scream*, you'll see how.) By then he had served ten years in Broadmoor and, believe me, it had taken its toll on him. He was down from twenty-plus stone to about thirteen stone, like a skeleton. His face was drawn and pale, his eyes bulging mad! Broadmoor was fucking hard on him! Injections! Solitary! Electric shocks! Pain and more pain! Even giants scream!

Frank Butler was another Broadmoor inmate. At one time Ron thought he was a friend but he turned out to be a right slag. He served eighteen years and got out and he went home to live in Newcastle. The prick started making calls to Kate Kray – insulting calls, degrading, frightening ... the filthy rat was a perv! It all came out eventually ... he had a history of indecent assaults and attacks on young girls! The eighteen years he had spent in Broadmoor were for cutting the tendons in the back of a young girl's legs! Evil fucker! Anyway, he ended up back inside. I hoped I'd bump into the reptile. Ronnie slipped up there!

It put the shits up Kate, but that type always get what's coming to them: a nasty end! I love to hear them scream! No woman deserves such filth down the phone!

That Stockwell Strangler (Ernestine) was on Ron's

ward! One evil rat! He killed about eight old people, buggered them too! After I left, some right monsters came to the place.

Ron would mark their card: 'Look away or I'll do you!'

Me, I'm afraid if I slip into them, I could not do time with such filth! My life in Broadmoor was solitary, so I had none of that. Fuck that! It's bad enough living with the muggy screws and doctors in your face, let alone the monsters.

CHAPTER 5

CRAZY MEMORIES

I remember I was in the seg block (isolation cells) in Wandsworth Jail, in 1976, when my granddad's house blew up in Rowley Road in Luton; it was the old gas boiler. Granddad was in bed when the roof blew off. What a way to go! Around the same time, I received my divorce papers, so I was in bits. Blown away!

I moved back to Parkhurst and it was Ronnie who helped me over that period of doom, because I was at my worst. Very dangerous. It is bad enough losing a loved one when your fate is double bad, especially when you're in a fucking big hole, and the hole was swallowing me up. Ron told me a lot about death and how best to face it, how to ride it and how to overcome it. A lot of what he said will be with me until my curtains come down. A lot is too personal to repeat, but so much of it made sense.

Those chats helped me become the man I am today. Death to me is just the start of things to come. Why worry about it? Why let it chew you up? Ron's philosophy was simple: 'Take it when it comes!'

When my granddad's roof blew off, it was his time. Like a squashed cat in the road, time was up for him. Shovel up the mess and get on with it.

The divorce? Fuck it! Shit happens!

Since then, I have lost so many people it is now just a matter of time as to who is next to pop off. This is how life is. Here today, gone tomorrow.

When you live our sort of lives or take our journey, you have to be prepared to lose 'everything'! You have to become a wolf.

I remember when I was on C Unit, in Parkhurst, Reg got me a pair of black and white boxing shoes, the best pair of gym boots I ever had. Ron got me black silk shorts with white stripes, the best boxing shorts ever. Terry Downes, the great boxer, sent me in some gloves! I later met him in Broadmoor (1981) on a visit Ron fixed up.

Some other Parkhurst memories: I recall a lifer named Ginger who had two budgies called Ron and Reg! Until Ron said, 'Change their names or bury them.' Ginger changed their names to Bonnie and Clyde.

Big Stevie Lannigan and some IRA pulled the roof off A Wing.

Big Albert Baker took a screw hostage in the seg unit.

Winnie McGee took over D Wing.

Nobby Clarke arrived from Broadmoor after being acquitted on a murder in Broadmoor. He was put on C Unit with us.

I spat in the evil child killer Ian Brady's face in the seg unit.

In fact, I lost a good three hundred days' remission in 1976! Mostly through assaults on scum. As you can see, 1976 was a lively year in Parkhurst!

Even in '76, the twins had their own Gillette razors, aftershaves and creams, sprays, their own mugs, china plates and bowls, Persian rugs, silk curtains and bedspreads. They had slippers, dressing gowns (with the 'RK' label on them) like smoking jackets. Their mother used to bring it all up on her visits. In those days, you could have it all brought or posted in.

My cell was bare, which is how I like it best! Ninety per cent of my stuff is permanently in a box under the bed (awaiting another a move). I cannot make a cell a home. I hate it! A cell is a cell to me.

Our kitchen was short of pots and pans. Ron had a crate of kitchen stuff sent in and donated it to C Unit for all. One day, a dozen two-litre flasks came in. Ron got everybody a flask. He would do things like that out of the blue, to cheer us all up.

On visits they both used to shake our visitors' hands and have a chat – always friendly to everyone. The singer Johnny Mathis had a number-one single that year with 'When a Child is Born'. Ron predicted it would be a number one, and it was. And the twins weren't forgotten on the outside: Steve Marriott, who had been the singer with The Small Faces, used to send the twins a lot of records to give to their friends, all signed.

Ron loved cheese on toast with spring onions. And both the twins ate their own garlic, which was grown in Parkhurst allotments by the lads.

Freddie Sewell, the cop killer, had his own greenhouse and grew the best tomatoes on the Isle of Wight. His corn on the cob was the best in the UK.

Hey, get this for a laugh! In Steve Wraith's book he says he was on a visit seeing Ronnie in Broadmoor and Ron asked him to bump somebody off. Now let's get real. Wraith, at the time, was just a kid. Ron was a major force in the underworld and he has asked Wraith to do this hit – out of ALL the people Ron knew he asked this one person to do a hit?

Let me put it right, now. He never did, nor would ever do, such a thing, apart from as a joke. So why does Wraith say such things, and write them? I will tell you why. To fill up pages. But that sort of shit destroys the Krays. People read it, believe it, then say what an evil bastard Ron must have been to ask such a thing of someone like Wraith.

Ron had chaps to do such acts, make no mistake about it. He wouldn't need a fucking idiot to do it, or someone like Wraith. And anyway, Wraith, why say such a thing now that he is dead? The difference between you and me is that I would have seen it as an honour to do such a bidding if I were free to have done so. Strange he never asked me to do anything like that, so why ask you? I rest my case.

Another crazy fact. I am the only man alive who can say I was jumped on by them both at the same time. Fortunately for me, they did so in good will so as to stop me from losing the plot. But that must be a one-off. Who else can say that? I'm only sad that their brother Charlie was not there, so I could have claimed the three Kray brothers did it! Now that could have gone in the *Guinness Book of Records* to add to my achievements.

* * * * *

In the 1970s and early Eighties, we could have toiletries sent in, along with trainers and clobber. I used to get a parcel every month sent in. Soaps, toothpaste, shampoo, Gillette razors, etc. Sadly it stopped, owing to mugs using this as a cover to smuggle in drugs. The same thing happened with food parcels for remands. We used to get all that. Again, down to drugs being smuggled in, it all stopped. Cons actually fuck up a lot of the system. But the ones who do it are the ones you hear crying in their pillows at night.

It was 1976 when Ron lost the plot over his toiletry parcel. For some reason, security stopped his pot of Brylcreem. They gave him everything else, but denied him his beloved hair cream.

I had just come out of the gym when I saw Ron shouting and screaming outside the office with half a dozen screws around him. I ran over to see what was going down. Ron stormed off and grabbed a fire bucket filled with sand. (On the end of C Wing we had about six buckets of sand near the firebox.)

Ron slung the bucket and the screws ran into the office. The alarm bell went off; Reg was trying to calm Ron down as scores of screws ran out the wing, some with sticks drawn. You must remember, this wing was notorious for trouble – not a week went by without some sort of violent incident. As it turned out, the matter was soon resolved and the Brylcreem was given to him. All that over some mug stopping him having what he was allowed. Ron did love his Brylcreem! I suppose, it's like the lads today with their hair gel.

Ron only used a toothbrush for a month and then got a new one. The average man has a toothbrush for years, Ron had twelve a year. That is how he was, he loved new stuff. If his shirt was missing a button, he would throw it away. He used a clean towel every day. Most cons have one a week.

But once in Broadmoor, where privileges were a hundred times better, Ron's quality of life improved. If he wanted ten towels a day, he got them. Clean bed sheets every day, good food, smart fresh clean clothes; he lived the life of a lord. Make no mistake about it, Broadmoor was his castle, he was the king.

Ron didn't go out into the exercise yard for fresh air for years in Broadmoor – he used to walk up and down the landing instead. Imagine that: years and years of never going out for some air. No wonder he had a grey complexion – prison pallor – walking up and down those asylum corridors, in his Savile Row suits and Gucci shoes. Thinking about life outside, dreams. How fucking cruel does it get? Years and years of fucking emptiness, being ripped up and dehumanised. Who said hanging is wicked? It would be a bloody relief, the final release.

Why don't they just shoot people who have no hope left? It would be more humane, surely. It is a great shame people outside cannot have a day in Broadmoor just to see the despair in the place. You can even smell it on the air. It stinks of misery and broken men crawling the walls. There must be a billion tears in that place! All dried up long ago.

A bag of fucking sweets and staring into space ... forever space ... slowly walking to your grave – what a way to go. Thank God I blew out of that hole. Phew! But writing about it now sure does bring it all back.

I have watched Ron, almost studied him. Eyes, look, stare, stance, attitude and walk. Let me tell you, he was a special sort of guy. Unique is the word. Ask anybody who visited Ron in his last years, let's say his last ten years alive. Nobody could ever tell me he was not unique, because I've never known anybody like him. How the fuck he survived all those years in that hellhole is beyond me. The psychological damage alone must have been torture. All of that, knowing he was doomed. How does a man get things each new day knowing the light will go out forever in a nut house?

As I write this, I hear Frank Bruno fell off the edge. It goes to show all the wealth and riches don't stop madness taking over. Good luck in your recovery, Frank. Fight it, because it will be your hardest ever fight! Not many overcome it, either.

There is a very thin line between being a genius and a lunatic, believe it. Look at Hitler, look at Stalin, look at Saddam Hussain: all fucking nuts ... but geniuses.

I remember once at Parkhurst, we had all been out on the yard sunbathing. The twins, me, Cubby, Chilly and a few others, when Ron just starts laughing, I mean really laughing! He couldn't fucking stop. Reg shouted, 'Shut up, Ron!' But it made him laugh more, then Chilly started, and, within five minutes, everybody was laughing, even Reg. We were all laughing, crying with laughter. Strange times. No sense in it. Total madness at its best. But what a memory. Imagine it, all out in the sun, then all laughing, but nobody knows why.

Believe me, prison can and does affect people; you have to be mad to overcome it.

Ron's laugh was infectious. His face used to screw up and his eyes bulged. You only had to look at him and hear him and you would laugh too. It was brilliant. But! That laugh could stop as fast as it started and end up nasty! Ron used to turn on strangers, new cons or new screws, and when he was on edge, tension was in the air. Reg stopped an amazing amount of violence. He must have been under a lot of stress with Ron, as he just did not know what was around the corner. Imagine it. It is bad enough in jail, without having to keep defusing violent situations.

We had our own seg block at the end of C Wing – four isolation cells – so when we got nicked and got any punishment, we would do it there. Ron had quite a few spells there. I was on there a few times with him, both on punishment. He used to walk up and down his cell a lot. At night, we used to have a chat through the gap in the doors. Ron used to always say, 'Goodnight, God bless and watch the bed bugs.'

* * * * *

Back then, prison nosh was the pits: stodge and plates of muck! We used to liven up our prison nosh by adding some sweetcorn. Knock up a bit of curry powder, get some oxo cubes. All those cheap things can spice the meal up.

Take a bowl of porridge, we'd add some nuts and raisins, a bowl of rice, or custard; cut up an apple or an orange, save the skin and squash it in hot water, it makes a wonderful, healthy drink. Prison duff (pudding) is tasteless shit. We'd add some honey to it or jam to liven it up; it would make it delicious.

Most jails have all those bits and pieces in the canteen. Some jails have gardens, so you can grow your own. You use lots of pepper and salt on your meals. Mayonnaise is a good buy too, and obviously sauces spice up meals. A good buy is stewing steak, which used to be 20p a tin. You just heat it up, and throw it in with the prison stew; a good meal that is. Plenty of protein in it.

Baked beans are only 40p a tin, you cannot go wrong with that. Even if you're a poor sod with little, you can always sort out a few tins! Or you can buy baccy and swap it for food: half an ounce gets you some prats' desserts for a week, or their weekend nosh. Some mugs would sell their own granny for a fag or some tack. Noodles are also a good buy, only cheap, 29p a pot. Filling too.

You have to use your head. Make it work for you. Survive. Ron's cupboard was always full to overflowing with extras in the line of goodies. He knew how to look after himself, food-wise; it was the fags what killed him!

* * * * *

Can you imagine the changes in prison life in the last three decades? Take it from me, it's a 'New World'. Different home secretaries and prison ministers, all have different ideas, some good, and some bad; some just totally insane!

I think, during my time inside, the worst home secretary was Michael Howard – and bear in mind, over the years, I've known some. Willie Whitelaw, Leon Brittan, now those two were evil! But Howard was worse! And he's the guy waiting to seize power from

Blair! The man of (Kack, er ... Jack) Straw is a joke: you only have to look at him and you can read him like a Beano book; a joke.

I laugh at jail 'incidents'. In Belmarsh, in 1996, during one breakfast on the Cat A Unit, this low-power (armed robber) young guy in his late twenties, a big lad, was in front of me in the queue and he blew me away with what he said. I could not believe what I heard, he was moaning about his boiled egg: 'Oi! Cunt, I'm not eating that – look at the shape of it. Get me another one.'

I looked at him, grabbed the egg, and said, 'I'll have it, I don't care if it's a square egg! What fucking odds does it matter what shape it is!'

I have never spoken to him again, simply because he is what I call a 'joke'. But it turns out he wasn't such a clown, as he won his trial and walked out!

Another incident at Belmarsh, in 1996: I got the hump with this Yardie mug (well, he acted the part), but he was a complete joke! This night he went on and on and on, music blazing away, shouting about me.

I banged and said, 'Give it a rest!' It was 2.30am, he was taking a real liberty. The mug had no respect for anyone, not even himself, a typical crackhead! I killed him a hundred times in my head. He had to have some!

I bided my time with it, as I wanted him badly. It came to a head in the washing-machine room. Belmarsh has those big industrial-size washers; only one con can use it on each wing (it's their job to do all the washing).

I hit this crackhead with a mop bucket. Crash! Then,

I stuffed him in the washer! It was just a lucky couple of minutes – no eyes, only one con up in there. I just said, 'Go.' Then the washer con came in with a pile of laundry, 'Turn it on, mate.' (I never had a clue how to work it.) He saw the waster inside and went pale!

'Fuck me, Chaz, I can't do that.'

'Why?'

'Well, he'll drown!'

'So what?'

'Blimey, Chaz, don't put that on me. I'm in enough trouble with my trial!'

So I pulled the waster back out and give him a few more thumps and left him lying in the laundry basket! I got a pull over it! But it turned out I done the wing a favour, as he was a pest. That's how it is in jail.

But it's all changed nowadays. I personally feel like a fish out of water, it's all kids' stuff these days – psychological, when before, it was physical.

Remember, there were no women working in male prisons three decades back. Now we have women governors, women screws and women welfare officers, even women chaplains! With smiles. Sweet smells. It's not prison, is it? Prison is supposed to be hard! 'Retribution', not smiles and comfort.

You can't have a decent punch-up today! When I first came in, you couldn't have radios; now they've got colour TVs. We had piss pots; now it's toilets. We had no light switches in cells; now they have switches and plug points! We had no choice of diet; now they have several!

We wore overalls and boots; now it's own clothes! I could go on and on about it – it's such a massive change.

Even homosexuality is allowed! Now, Ron would have loved that! In some jails they give out condoms to the male cons – it's true! Don't it make you sick! It could not have happened thirty years ago, but through it all I still live in the past, as my world is still solitary.

In the odd times I do get up on a wing, you will know now why it is I go mad! It's the mugs I have to live with. 'Sir, there's a lump in my porridge.' 'Sir, I've got no condoms and my pad mate wants to give me a good seeing to.' 'Sir, Sir, Sir!' Cor, do me favour! Bring back the birch, let's all have a whip round, I say!

Bread and water! Prisons are full of paedophiles, full of sex monsters, full of weak people, grasses, drug mugs! Get me out of here; I'm nearly a celebrity! It's crawling under my skin. Why can't I have a sleeping bag and do my time up on a roof away from it all! In fact, why don't you set me free?

* * * * *

Here's a funny thing that will blow your socks off! Did you know Reggie and me proposed to the same woman? Yeah, it's a fact! It was in about 1993; I bet you can't guess who it was. Well, if you get Kate Kray's book *Free At Last*, you'll see who. Get her book! I'll keep it a secret. But I'll tell you now, its one hundred per cent true!

She's a lifer. The press labelled her the Black Widow,

but I changed that, it's now the Black Rose! She got life for allegedly shooting Ronnie Cooke. His face got blown off with a twelve-bore sawn off.

Ronnie Cooke was a top blagger, if not the best! He was serving eighteen years over a van! He gets to the end, has a bit of home leave and ... bang, he's on the slab with no head left! A fucking sad end! But that's the life we live, a violent life mostly ends violently! The Black Rose got life; she still fights for her innocence.

Anyway, around 1993, I used to phone her once a month, a little perk I had for being good. She was up in Durham H Wing.

During one phonecall, I said out of the blue, 'Hey, let's get married.' The phone went silent. 'Er, did you hear me?'

'Yeah, Charlie, I'm sorry, I can't.'

'Oh, yeah?' I said. 'Well, if you won't marry me, then I'll have to stick to my apple pies and Bertha!'

'Who?' she said.

'Bertha! She's my eighteen-pound medicine ball; we broke a world record together! In Belmarsh Jail, 1995!'

Now, the same week, Reg proposed to her – how or why is beyond me! But he did and she said 'no' to him as well! (You can't please some women.) But let me tell you all, she's a diamond, a true East Ender. Solid! We all love the Black Rose – we respect her. I'd say she's now served about thirteen years. Personally, for what it's worth, I don't believe she blew Ron Cooke away. And one day it will all come out.

Did you know, Reg and Charlie Kray were both friends with Barbara Windsor? And Reg used to take Judy Garland out. Every time she was over here in the Sixties, she dined with Reg! I once went out with Lilly 'Legs' Lovelace. Who? Yeah, you may well ask! (Best you don't.) Let's just say she had legs that went right up to her neck!

I once went to Caesers Palace to see Shirley Bassey. I've idolised her ever since. What a voice, what a star! Why can't people respect her for what she is? Our top star of all time! It's the same old story; people won't realise how good she is till she's dead – just as it was with Dusty Springfield and Roy Orbison. When our greats die, people say, 'Cor, he/she was good!' Well, start now, Shirley Bassey is GREAT! The soppy Spice Girls couldn't clean her shoes!

CHAPTER 6

JACK PALANCE?
NAH – CHARLES BRONSON

I'd just taken two hostages and was talking to a member of my family on the phone. 'LET THEM GO, NOW!' they told me. Like a prat, I did. And the screws came in with the liquid cosh injection and slung me in a van!

I woke up in Risley remand centre – after eleven-and-a-half years; I had come full circle and was back to square one! Risley was for remands at that time, it dealt with the Liverpool and Manchester areas. To say I was sick of it would have been an understatement!

I had only been there a few days when I saw the fat rat, Murray, a slag from Parkhurst Jail. Well, he was now on remand for murder – he'd sexually assaulted and killed three young lads. I got myself a nice tool and I was all set to serve him up his just desserts, but he must have said something to the screws, as I was moved away from him to a new wing. He ended up with a life sentence with a recommendation that he serve thirty years. Let's hope he dies. I can't see why we can't top slags like him – what good is he alive? All sex beasts should be topped!

Anyway, the twins supported me in Risley, and so did Charlie Kray. Parcels came in droves: mugs and clothes. I'd break a watch; a new replacement watch would arrive. I'd break a radio, and a new one would come in the post.

My life in Risley was crazy. It was hard for me after having been locked up for so long. All these guys around me were new in off the streets! Even the clothes they wore looked strange. So it was no wonder I was forever involved with trouble! Not a week went by when I wasn't involved in a punch-up of some sort – but I love a row, so it suited me! A good fight helps you keep on your toes and clears the air! I hit one guy so fucking hard, I broke my hand. Fuck me, he had a hard head!

My old buddy, Craig Bulger, came up to visit me. A great guy is Craig, a top Manchester lad! Then I met Andy Vassel there, a life-long pal.

I remember one morning, I was slopping out (it was all piss pots in them days). Some screw upset me, so I slung the lot all over him! That was it for me in Risley, it was war after that! Those screws up North don't mess about!

I believe at this time in my life that I was on a mission of madness. A journey of destruction, with no brakes. Fuck me, I never even had a steering wheel! I was just waiting to crash!

Top: Early days. The twins when they were still identical, fighting fit and embracing their beloved mother.

Bottom: You've got to stay tough inside. Reg always kept himself in shape and at fifty had the body of a young man. The message says, 'Charlie, God bless, your friend Reg.' A diamond.

In the company of giants.

Top: (from right) Freddie Foreman, Reggie and Charlie relax with British boxing Henry Cooper (*second from left*).

Bottom: Reggie and Ronnie meet boxing legend Joe Louis. The twins had huge respect for boxing and were both accomplished fighters.

Me and the twins used to spar to keep us fit and on our toes – the only way to cope with the madness! Here, I keep the tradition going with great pal Tony Mcullough, in Hull Prison. (*Bottom left*) The lads and I give con-killer Fred Lowe a lift.

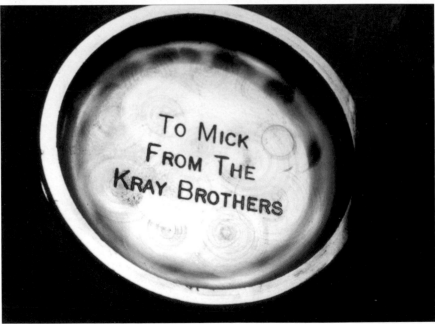

TO MICK
FROM THE
KRAY BROTHERS

Prized possessions. Here's the beautiful pocket watch given to me by the twins before I changed my name. It's just one of the numerous generous gifts I received from Ronnie and Reggie over the years. There's also my sunglasses, now a Bronson trademark – I don't know where I'd be without them!

Though we were often moved around the country, we always stayed in touch. (*Clockwise from top left*) A letter from Ron in Broadmoor, 1994, telling me to stay out of trouble – good advice! Charlie thanks me for my letters and Reg's scrawl wishes me well. Touching stuff, eh!

Some of my prize-winning artwork, dedicated to the twins.

Top: Ron expressed himself by painting in prison – he did this lonely landscape in Broadmoor. Now his pictures go for thousands of pounds.

Bottom: Fifty years on and people are still fascinated by the twins – the number of books and amount of memorabilia is staggering. This is just a fraction of it from a private collection.

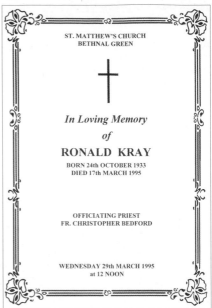

Top left: Ron's marriage to Kate Kray in 1990 was one of the happiest days of his life.

Top right: Ron's funeral service brought the East End to a standstill – thousands turned out to pay their last respects.

Bottom: This wreath at Reggie's funeral just about sums it all up. The twins were men of honour, and they got the recognition they deserved. RIP.

One day, the screws just crashed into my cell, for no reason – it was simply payback time. They just steamed into me, like an out-of-control locomotive.

I shouted, 'If that's the best you slags can do, why bother!'

After that, it was very tense – they were flapping! Some even tried to be nice, but it was too late for that! I was spitting on them just for the sake of it, just waiting for my chance. One slip-up and I'd claim one. They knew it!!

Eventually, my court case came up at Liverpool Crown Court. I appeared in front of Judge Temple, a nice old chap. He was fair to me. OK, if he'd given me ten years then I wouldn't be saying these nice things about him, but he was a sensible judge. I was given three years, which for such serious charges was a great result.

My next stop was Walton Jail, in Liverpool. But, when you're such a face as I am, you're lost before you arrive. I've dug my own hole. It started as soon as I arrived! They were there waiting, a reception committee of hard-faced screws. I was smashed up and put in the box; they took no chances! Soon after that, I got up on their roof and smashed it up. That cost me another year on top of what I had already got.

So my journey went on: jail to jail, block to block, my life was one long journey of punishment. In one year, I moved eighteen times! Nobody wanted me: Leeds, Durham, Hull, Strangeways, Walton, Winson Green, Winchester, Wandsworth, the Scrubs, Albany, Gartree,

Bristol and on and on. Then, I'd start back at the beginning again. It became a vicious circle of pain. (If I wasn't mad in Broadmoor, I sure was now!)

I was 21 years old when I got put inside; I was now in my mid-thirties. But, through it all, I kept my strength – my press-ups and sit-ups were second to none. I rarely got to use a gym, so I worked out in my cell! I was fast, fit and powerful, and all I had to sustain me was shit food and bad treatment!

The inevitable happened. I hit Parkhurst again: early in 1986, they put me on B Wing! Guess what? Yeah, Reg was on there! It had been eight years since I'd last seen him and he looked fucking brilliant – fit and well. He was alive and kicking, working out in the gym, really doing magic!

I had only been on the wing a couple of days when Henry Farrell arrived. Now I like Henry, but not many did, as he was very unpredictable, ex-Broadmoor. I knew how to relate to him; others didn't.

I had a word with him to calm down and relax, but he went off it, rushing around upsetting people. And one of the people he upset was Reg, but, unlike me, Reg didn't understand his strange ways. It turned out nasty and Reg went in and chinned him, kicked him clean out. I said to Reg, 'I'll sort it.' Reg left and I helped Henry come round. Poor sod, he never knew where he was or what happened.

'You OK, mate?' I asked him.

'Yeah, yeah.'

But, days later, didn't he go and upset another con and he got it again. I told Henry the way he was going he was likely to get weighed in. In fact, soon after this, he left the wing and did his bird in the hospital. Years of the asylum had fucked him up. It was sad, but there were a lot of cons like Henry. They're just puzzled. But I have that special quality where I can help them; others don't have it. I actually feel sad for them – they're like a fish out of water.

At this time, Reg was having it with a young con. Few liked this geezer, as he was a flash fucker. He was a 'nobody', but when he got to Parkhurst, and after meeting Reg, he thought he was a 'somebody'. People were laughing at him. But he made Reg happy, so he had his merits.

At this time, Parkhurst was buzzing with good people: Alec Sears, Charlie Knight, Siddy Draper, Bob Maynard and Martin Long, all great guys! Then it went off and I attacked a screw and a governor and got moved out.

It was while I was away that a big punch-up went off down the field and Reg was involved. It happened over this young geezer, he got flash on the football pitch and it went off, every fucker was throwing punches. Ray Baron, a South London armed robber, hit Reggie. Reg never forgot it.

At this time, I was in a dungeon in Wandsworth. I've spent a lot of my time in dungeons over the years. After a spell there, I moved to the Scrubs block and, lo and behold, Reg was there! The van that dropped me off took Reg back to Parkhurst, but before he left he told me about Baron getting in a sly punch. 'Fuck him,' I told Reg, 'he's only a cunt!'

So, Reg went back to Parkhurst and I stayed in the Scrubs for a spell. Well, until I dived on the governor and started to strangle him. I was soon moved out. Wonder why ...

I was back on the merry-go-round again: block to block, till finally I landed back in Parkhurst. A week before I got there, Reg had moved to Gartree. He had spent almost eighteen years at Parkhurst.

I bumped into Ray Baron in Parkhurst and punched his fat face in. I then had a run in with the scumbag Tommy Mulligan who had attacked my pal George Heath; Mulligan later hanged himself in his cell.

It was around this time that Graham Young died in Parkhurst and Alex Hessen; both were natural lifers! Young was Britain's number-one poisoner. He first poisoned his family when he was fifteen years old, killing two of them. After that, he was sent to Broadmoor. Twenty years later, they let him out and he poisoned his workmates; another two died! Evil bastard! Hessen killed an inmate in Maidstone; he was a crazy fucker – dangerous!

I went back on the move. I bumped into Harry Johnson in Leicester block. Harry was a legend. The twins loved him, called him 'Hate 'em All Harry'. They got Harry a gold Rolex watch for cutting George Ince in

Long Lartin Jail. Ince was a rat. He went with Dolly Kray (Charlie's wife) while Charlie was serving his ten-year sentence. Sure, it takes two to tango, but you just don't do that sort of thing! Ince needed 100 stitches to sew his face back together. Harry got more years added, but, fair play, Ince tried to get Harry off with it!

Later, Ince got a twelve-bore stuffed down his trousers and was shot. He survived! Harry served twenty years in jail, all to die an old man. He was a fearless man, and loved a rip-up! He stuffed a china mug in McVicar's face up in Durham unit, in the 1960s. In a nutshell, he had a fight with anyone who was anyone. 'Hate 'em All' was a right fucking handful.

It was Ronnie Kray who gave him the 'Hate 'em All' name. It happened on the unit in Parkhurst in the early 1970s. Harry had just put a dumbbell in Billy Skingle's head. After that, he was in his cell arguing with himself in the mirror. Ron said, 'Fuck me, he hates everybody, including himself.' 'Hate 'em All' was born.

The people I bumped into on my travels! I just could not get away from the Krays. Even screws would ask, 'How's the twins?' 'Where are they now?'

As a governor in Wandsworth was doing the rounds one time, he said to me – in front of all the block screws – 'You're too much like the Krays, you are.'

I said, 'Which one?'

He replied, 'All of them!'

I said, 'What's the problem then?'

He mumbled something incomprehensible in reply

and left. I shit him up the next day! I was soon moved.

It was now early 1987 – thirteen years since I had come inside! Fucking thirteen years! Not one day had I been out! I was still a Cat A prisoner, still labelled a danger! My life was now solitary – that was all I knew. Somebody from Prison Service H/Q came to see me. He told me I was to be moved to Gartree Jail and stay there till my release on 30 October 1987, adding that I would spend my time there on the block in solitary and that I would be released straight from Cat A. I said, 'Big deal, let's go.'

I arrived at Gartree and found myself in the block. I could finally see the end! I was going home in eight months' time – and Reg was in Gartree! He was up on the wing. I pulled the governor the next day and put a deal to him: 'Let me see Reg once a week and I'll settle down, you won't know I'm here.' He had a meeting on it and agreed. I would remain in solitary, but I could go down the field on a Sunday to see Reg. I also got three sessions in the gym. But any fucking about and I would lose the lot. I was well happy. Life was looking good! For the first time in nearly fourteen years, I could plan my future. I was going home! I was like a little boy at Christmas – yeah, I had won!

My routine began, a bit of gym, a chat with Reg once a week, and boxing it clever. At this time, Gartree was full of great guys: Johnny Kendall, Charlie McGhee, Steve Waterman, Roy Walsh, Rocky Lee, Mickey Hammad, Harry Roberts. But Reg was my best pal. We would have a walk and a chat; he was made up for me!

I was in the best shape of my life. Lots of fruit, food, and gym! I was 210 pounds and solid muscle; strong, fit and fast!

One time, Reg said to me, 'Okay, what are you going to do on the outside?' The truth is, I never had a clue! I had never even thought about that. 'What will I do?' I replied. 'Probably rob a bank.'

Reg stopped still, looked at me and said, 'No, you don't want to do that, don't do it! Look, why don't you do some fights, be a boxer? You're fit, you don't smoke, don't do drugs; you're only 36! I'll help you get started!'

And that's how it happened. Reg got a fight promoter, Paul Edmunds, to get in touch with me. Eventually, Paul – from Canning Town, London – came up to see me, we chatted, and did a deal! There was just one problem: I had to have an alias name, so we spent half the visit, deciding on a name for me! We both agreed that my fighting name would be 'Charles Bronson', although Paul did suggest the name Jack Palance.

I was now an unlicensed fighter and trained the rest of my bird away. I got super fit; I skipped; I did bag work, sit-ups, circuits; I even sparred with some of the lads in the gym. I was to be freed on 30 October; my first fight was 12 November, which took place above a pub in East London. 'Bronson' was born – to fight!

In the meantime, Paul attempted to get me a pro-licence from the British Board of Boxing Control. Sadly, I was refused on the grounds of being a certified madman, and ex-Broadmoor! So I was unlicensed. 'Fuck it, who needs a licence, that's for fairies and taxpayers – I'm a birdman!'

I got a nice letter from Ronnie wishing me well. He had also sent me a grand and told me to enjoy myself! I was weeks away from freedom; I could not wait!

By now, Reg had served nineteen years. I felt fucking sad to think about it. Here he was, worrying about me; he was so excited for me – it was as if it was his future, not mine. He said he would have a nice few bob on me to win! I said, 'Put all you've got on me to win. I can't lose!' Even if my opponent came at me with a gun, I knew I would win! All those years of frustration bottled up, I was like a powder keg … ready to blow!

So it was set, I was going home! But where was home? A big slice of my life had been eaten away by the years I had served, but I actually felt sad that I was leaving Reg behind. At that time he had eleven more years out of his thirty-year tariff to serve, although, as it turned out, he was to serve in excess of the thirty years recommended for him. Ron was to die in Broadmoor. All my pals had years left to serve. I felt like I was running out on them!

Fuck it; I had to win for them! I walked out of Gartree a free man; in my black suit I was about to explode!

Two nights before the fight, I arrived at Canning Town and stayed with Paul's mum! She was a diamond – all his family are. I met them and they spoiled me rotten!

The night before the fight, I had a call from Reg and

Ron; it was about 7pm when Ron called to wish me well and said he had a nice bet on it.

I said, 'No problem, Ron – it's won!'

Then, Reg phoned about 7.30pm. 'Good luck,' he said. It blew me away!

Then at the fight itself, I saw Charlie Kray! He came over to have a word. I was buzzing and ready to explode – and I did! I never saw the man I was about to face as a fighter. I saw years of madness. I saw red! I wanted to fucking kill him! I was going insane! He had to go! He was an animal! His body was full of hair, and he had that sort of face you just can't wait to smash up! He was the copper with the gun in my face; he was the screw with the stick in his hand; he was the prison doctor who stitched me up with a blunt needle; he was everybody that ever fucked with my life! The judge, the grasses, the nosy probation officers, the slags who made me what I am. He was Broadmoor! He was that evil bastard who squeezed my balls! He had to have some! He was in my face!

'Ding, ding.'

I ran out and smashed him! I hit him with hooks, crosses and combinations! Even when he fell, I was still smashing into him. I felt his ribs snap. I felt his face open up … I was laughing … I lost control … I was no longer in the ring … I was fighting in a nightmare for survival!

I had others on top of me, strangling me, bending my arms! Dragging me off … shouting … more abuse! They were pulling me off the animal. I thought it was screws again. I had lost my mind! It took me a good five minutes to compose myself, to calm my mind! I watched the pool of blood, where he lay in a heap! I had won! It was over!

I said to Paul, 'Get me another, soon!'

He said, 'Sorted.'

Charlie came up to me and said, 'Awesome.'

The fight was videoed; he promised the twins would get to see it! Ron would love it!

I showered and left. I had won my sanity! I was free from madness ... but for how long?

Thanks to Reg and Ron's support, I was now free and winning. And I would win again! All I had to do was psyche myself up and think of the past! How could I lose, it was easy!

Fight number two happened on 3 December 1987. I was to fight Gypsy Joe, a man who had won his last ten fights! This contest was going to be a bit harder than the last one. This geezer was a big guy, 230 pounds, though with a bit of a belly. He looked like what he was: a hard man!

But not for one minute did I believe that I would lose. I told Paul to get me a winner-take-all. Gypsy Joe snapped at it – in his head he was unbeatable!

I knew I had to play this one smart. I borrowed three grand and put it on myself to win at 2/1. Plus the winnings would be mine ... well, it beats doing a blag on a bank!

'Ding, ding.'

Crash! He was a tough cookie! He gave as good as he got! But, after the bell, I knew I had him in round two. He was puffing and panting; I wasn't even in a sweat! I said to my corner men, 'This is it, it's all over for him!'

'Ding, ding.'

Crash! I caught him such a body blow, I felt my fist reach inside and smash against his spine, that was it … the rest was simple. I threw about another twenty punches after that body blow, at least fifteen in his face. I had three of his teeth embedded in my right glove. He was out cold! I looked down at him, and all I saw was a sack of shit! It meant nothing to me! I could have chopped off his head and kicked it into the crowd – it meant nothing! I shouted to the crowd, 'That one's for the twins!' Paul was buzzing!

My third fight was on 22 December. Could you see Bruno fighting so many fights in such a short space of time! I was no sooner out of the ring than I was back in! I loved it – it was my escape.

The night before the third fight, Ron and Reg phoned me at Paul's to wish me well. Charlie popped in to wish me all the best too. I told him to put a nice few bob on me to win. He smiled, and said, 'I've done that.'

'Ding, ding.'

I couldn't lose! I was on a run – and it wasn't because of good luck!

* * * * *

After being free for 69 days, on 7 January 1988, it all came to an end. My world fell in on me! I ended up with a dozen men on top of me, bashing me to bits! To cut a long story short, I was charged with armed robbery on a jeweller's. And, to make matters worse, the police took the piss and charged me in the name of 'Charles Bronson'.

I was back inside – this time, in Leicester Jail. Would you believe it, Harry 'Hate 'em All' Johnson was in the next cell to me on the block! He thought it was funny, me with the name Bronson on my door!

My fucking head was in bits! I just could not believe it! It felt like a dream, like I had never been out! I kept asking myself, 'Why? Why did I rob the jeweller?' The answer was simple: I'm a villain. As much as Reg was born to be violent, I was born to rob. And I loved it! The excitement! Plus, I wanted a nice piece of Tom (jewellery) for some woman! Something special – fuck paying for it! Anyway it was no good crying, I was nicked! I was back inside and I just had to get on with it.

Andy Russell arrived in the jail around the same time. He had just got nicked for breaking Sid Draper and Johnny Kendall out of Gartree with a fucking helicopter! Britain's first ever escape with a chopper! (They'll make a movie about that one day.) Yeah, that was special!

It wasn't long before I started getting really fed up, and when I get fed up it's danger signs. So up I went – I do love a roof. I've been up on more prison roofs than

Santa! I would have been a great roofer! Needless to say, I was soon moved on, this time to Brixton D Special Unit (high risk). Well, it was till two IRA broke out with a gun. Got clean away, they did.

There was another bunch of great chaps in there, such as Ronnie Easterbrook, a good pal of the twins. I had last seen Ronnie at Parkhurst in 1976. He was now in real trouble after a spot of armed robbery and shooting at the pigs (for which he later got life). Then there was Tommy Hole Senior and Junior, father and son. Young Tom got nine years … and later, he hanged himself in Parkhurst. Old Tom got 22 years; he later won his appeal, but sadly was to die in a shooting in a pub in Canning Town. Two very sad deaths. Two great guys! Two dear friends!

Then there was Mickey Rielley. He got fourteen years for doing a bank. Dennis Wheeler, he got sixteen years for a bit of puff (well, OK, 25 tons of it!). There was Charlie McGhee – he got life for shooting a pig over a bit of work and later died in Frankland, a very sad loss. Charlie was from my home town. There was Perrie Warrie, he got life, and Wayne Hurren, he got twenty years for armed robbery.

The Dunford brothers, John and Andy – they got sixteen years for robberies. Yeah, some great guys, but one was an icon, the greatest robber I ever met: Valerio 'Gigi' Viccei (an Italian national). He was nicked for the Knightsbridge safety boxes – £60 million. Gigi, as he was known, had style and class – he was the guv'nor!

The £60 million says as much, but he was also a superb bank robber, the best. I loved this guy to bits! Sadly, he got twenty! He served eight years over here and was then taken back to Italy to finish his time off in one of their prisons. He won parole ... and then got shot dead by the pigs! A right sad ending.

I was kept in a cage in Brixton. Why? You tell me. They probably never trusted me! But one day, I got out and ripped into one of the IRA cons. I smashed him with a tea urn. Why? 'Cos I felt like it.

There was certainly some fun and games in Brixton while I was there. Big Ferdi stabbed up Charlie McGhee (not nice), but they sorted it out later! At one time, Ferdi was in serious trouble over it. He later got stabbed up himself, so it was quits. It's a funny old business this jail life, eh! We all love Ferdi now – top man!

Then big Vic Dark tried to escape. Now, this guy is a face in East London – well respected! He can have a right row, but sadly it got on top. He later got seventeen years for armed robbery; I would bump into Vic many times in different jails. Another top man.

Me, I ended up, would you believe, with another seven years, but bear in mind my last seven years meant that I ended up serving fourteen years. I think Judge Hickman gave me seven years so as to say, 'Do your time and go home or serve another fourteen years.' Take him down! Clang!

My first stop was Wandsworth. The bollocks started from day one with me! I bumped into Frank Fraser there. He was back in doing three years over some coins; Frank's a class guy, top man. Served over forty years' bird, been cat-'o-nine-tailed, birched, you name it. Frank is hard – and I mean, rock fucking hard. The twins loved Frank; we all do! Men like Frank are a dying breed – dinosaurs!

Wandsworth is a shithole, but you get to see loads of great guys. Big Del Croxen was there. Now he's a powerhouse, sixteen stone of beef! One hard bastard! But he later died in jail. He was only 37 years old – it was a fucking tragedy, broke my heart that did. I don't mind admitting, I cried! What a waste – he had two lovely kids, a nice wife and he died in jail! Life at times can be so cruel! He was a good villain was Del! One of the best! Staunch. Solid.

Dennis Campbell was there too, he copped seventeen years. Kevin Brown, a real block man, he got sixteen years. Kevin almost got out of Wandsworth in a JCB! But it failed and he got a terrible bashing. Kev plods on in his own little way; he's done all of his time the hard way. There's two ways to do something in life: the way others tell you to do it and the way you WANT to do it – Kev does it his way.

There were lots of faces, all top villains! Steve Davies, Johnny Hamilton, Mickey Moss, Terry Smith – I could go on all day! Eventually though, I started getting bored again. So I demolished my cell and served a screw up. It was time to move on!

Up in Full Sutton Jail, who did I bump into but

Freddie Foreman! Now, Fred's the 'godfather' of crime, and a strong pal of the Krays. I've known Fred for years, so it was a bonus to see him again. We had a Christmas together. Eddie Richardson was also up there; Eddie is a right nice fella. The faces I bump into! (A lot of rats too!) Yeah, on my travels I've met 'em all!! Anyone who's anyone, I've met!

Mickey McAvey (Brinx Matt); Big 'H' McKewley; Bruce Reynolds; Tommy Wisbey (great train robbers); Harry Roberts − 3 X cop killer; Fred Sewell − cop killer; Billy Skingle − cop killer; Neil Adamson − cop killer; Birmingham 6; Guilford 4; Winchester 3.

Fuck me, I was two cells away from Fred West in Winson Green (HMP Birmingham)! He looked like that silly fucker Benny out of Crossroads! He went and hanged himself − it was the best thing he ever done! Fucking nonce! It's a pity that slag Rose West wouldn't do it!

Yeah, I've met them all! Ronnie Knight, Charlie Knight, Johnny Knight, Kenny Noye, Billy Gentry, Alan Byrnes, Dave Courtney, Ian Durum, Steve Durum, Danny Alpress, Davy Cottage, Dave Martin, Joey Martin, Wally Lee, Sammy McCarthy, Frank Contek, Johnny Asa.

The twins were keeping contact with me as I flew through the system, from jail to jail! At times, they found it hard to keep up with me! But they always sorted me out. Often, out of the blue, I would get a £50 note from Ron, some books or mags off Charlie, or a letter off Reg. It all helps to keep a guy alive.

Reg finally came off Cat A – twenty years he was on it, that's one hell of a time! Then they moved him to Nottingham Jail, which is a Cat B training prison – a lot of lifers go there – but things went sour. Some cunt slipped a note in the box saying Reg was going to escape! It was so much bollocks. Why should he try and escape? What sense would there have been in that? Reg was a man who settled in serving his sentence; he had never tried to escape in twenty years, so why would he try now? He had the means to escape, he only had to say the word and he would have had an army of chaps breaking him and Ron out from behind bars. But they didn't want to be in the run and hunted down like animals. They wanted to be able to walk around and hold their heads up high.

The governor should have seen right through it. But Reg got moved back to Gartree! A lesser man would have cracked up and just lost hope, but not Reg: he got his lawyer on it and his MP and got it resolved – he proved it was all bollocks!

Reg's next visit was to Maidstone Jail – a good move! And there he settled for a good spell! His old mate Joey Martin was there, and John Heibner, so Reg was happy. Then, Freddie Foreman turned up – so it was just like old times!

Maidstone's got its own swimming pool, and with that, plus plenty of gym and punch bags, Reg kept in shape. The visits are better in a less secure jail too, so he got to see some of his old pals who he hadn't seen for years, like Joe Pyle, Roy Shaw, Lenny McLean – all top men! It was all good for him. Bear in mind, Ron had been allowed to see visitors like this since his Broadmoor move, so Reg was making up for lost time! Me, I kept myself on the move. Life for me was just more and more madness. I got myself in big trouble – prison was gradually driving me mad!

Then Ron went and did it again! He loved to shock and surprise people! He got married for a second time, this time to Kate, who had originally been a visitor to Reg. I'll put the record straight here, 'cos there's a lot of shit talked about it. Some say Kate married Ron for the money, others for the name, blah, blah, blah. Let me tell you now: it's not so. For starters, Kate probably had more money than Ron! She ran a Kissogram company and a chauffeuring business with Rolls-Royces. She was a top businesswoman, a very smart and clever lady!

Kate Kray was and is a lovely lady, and Ron idolised her. His whole world lit up with Kate; she gave him that sparkle. For most of his life, Ron really only ever loved his mum. I think Kate gave him back some humanity and warmth. Even Ron's letters seemed to be nicer – happier – after they got together, so it was a great relationship. And Kate's a diamond! You'll still get the mugs trying to pull her down. But they don't even know her or what Ron was all about; they read some shit story in the press and believe it. Well, take it from me, Kate's a top lady! They come no better!

* * * * *

I had a crazy brainstorm one day and took Governor Masserick hostage up in Frankland Jail. One insane day; it almost cost me a trip back to Broadmoor! I was actually warned that I was on thin ice! 'Slow down or you'll be nutted off!'

My journey was a hard one – I just could not settle! The longer I do, the harder it gets! But with Bronson on my door, it's almost impossible to walk away from it. It's in my face; there is no escape from it.

At times, I see no sense or sanity. I lose the plot and go mad; wherever I went, the screws seemed set on messing me about. I was forever chinning them; I did three in one day in Gartree, and three in Long Lartin. I was up on roofs. I was in all sorts of scraps! But let me tell you now (to all the Y/Ps out there reading this), think before you start to fight the system. You'll lose! All you'll gain is a name! The best idea is just to get out and go home. You can't win! How can you? Take it from me, you can't, all you get is pain and misery, so think about it. I'll say it again: do yourself a favour – behave and go home!

Every punch you throw in jail, you have to take twenty back. You can't have, or expect, a fair fight with a screw 'cos, if you beat him, his mates will join in. So how can you have a straight war? You can't!

A sad day for me came one time when I was back in Parkhurst! I had a fall-out with a London face, and it got nasty! Others joined in, and I got it in the back – four big holes! I was hurt badly! Blood was coming out of me like a tap! I was dying, bleeding to death, the life just gushing out of me. I woke up in St Mary's Hospital, on glucose and a blood drip; four holes in my back still can't put me away! But that's how close I came.

With me, it's like playing Russian roulette – I just don't care. Kill me, but expect to die with me, that's my motto! He who dares sometimes dies! But I'm still here! My body is a mass of scars, but I'm still in one piece. But I've got to keep my body going – bear in mind that ninety per cent of my time I spend in blocks, in solitary confinement or special units. I have to stop my body from slowing down with exercises, workouts.

When I was in Lincoln Prison, I chinned a governor. Hull, I took a governor hostage. All the max-secure jails: Long Lartin; Whitemoor; Gartree; Parkhurst; Frankland; Full Sutton; Woodhill unit and Belmarsh unit, I've had 'em all! Violence on top of violence, so much, it makes you feel sick. I've got to get the fuck out!

For some time I had a special civilian friend – Lord Longford. He would always put me in his books. Sadly, he's passed away now, but he used to travel to visit me all over the country, which was no mean feat for a man who was 94 when he died! (I just wish he hadn't wasted his time on that Myra Hindley when she was still around – she was a witch!)

My mum and dad used to visit me all through my years, loyalty that is second to none! I do not smoke or do drugs, so I need very little in jail; but a nice hug from my mum works wonders with me. My mum is my angel;

I adore her! My life ran to a strict regime of porridge, press-ups, sit-ups and a couple of visits each month. Don't sound much, does it, but to me, it was my life.

A lot of great pals have died during my time inside. A cell death is never easy! Like my old mate Tony Cunningham. On 14 December '85, I was walking around the exercise yard of Wandsworth Prison with Tony and another con called Noel Travis. It was bloody freezing. Tony was telling us a few jokes; he had us laughing. The very next day he hanged himself in his cell. He really broke my heart, he was a great guy, I liked him – it should never have happened! He was only serving seven years; he was so young and had a great life ahead. Why, can we ever know why, does it ever make sense? It just doesn't make sense. He chose to tell Noel and me his jokes rather than his problems, for that we must respect him but I wish he'd told us, I only wish. No letter, nothing. Why? What for! Who knows?

The one con I truly admire was David Martin. I met Dave in the block in Wandsworth Prison in the 70s; he was moved from Gartree after getting out of his cell and caught in the workshop. Whilst at Wandsworth Prison he cut his cell bars. He was forever trying to get away. He could make keys out of plastic knives, he was probably the most gifted of all the would-be jail breakers I've ever met. He later became Britain's most wanted man after escaping from a cop shop. The cops shot him, he shot them.

Later he was set up by a girlfriend and was caught in the London underground.

He received 25 years and finally hanged himself in the special unit in Parkhurst. I could never work out why he decided to take his life, as sure as day turns to night my money would've been on Dave to escape again. He was born a legend, lived a legend and died a legend. And Dave Martin hanged himself in Parkhurst too. A whole bunch of mates have hanged themselves: Mickey Jameson (Full Sutton); Dessy Cunningham (Whitemoor) – no relation to Tony; John Paton (Garth); John Bund (Parkhurst). Then there was Barry Rondeau (cut his throat) and Eddie Watkins (overdosed), both in Long Lartin. So many more! All tragic. All of them gave up on life.

I once saw a hanging up in Risley – I never forgot it, even the smell never leaves you! A prison suicide is, without a doubt, the most tragic way of leaving this life. Don't do it! Never lose your faith!

* * * * *

In rolled 1992. Eighteen years had now passed by since I entered jail, and for all but a poxy few weeks of freedom I had been caged up – and, in my case, 'caged' is the word! The majority of my time is spent in solitary. But it's now all I know! It's what I do best!

My release date was set for 14 November 1992. I was finally going home, I was forty years old, and still a very fit man! But in reality, I was going out to fuck all. I was considered a danger to society – I was actually told that I would be shot dead before the pigs would arrest me, as I was a threat to them! Every cop shop in the UK had my photo; every cop was warned I was getting out! I would be under 24-hour surveillance.

My last couple of weeks I spent in the Scrubs punishment block – alone, in deep thought! I had to try harder this time; I could not afford to return again. Enough was enough! I had to change my life.

So I arranged for a clean break. My pal, Mark Lilliott, sorted me out a flat up in New Brighton and a job on a club door. A fresh start! The time had arrived to be sensible and sane. And start acting my age! A new life!

The twins both sent me a good luck card; Charlie sent me in a few quid. I wrote and thanked them for all their support over the years, but now I intended to go straight. They were genuinely pleased for me. I felt I could do it. I believe, also, a lot of screws were pleased for me; I know the governors were, as they were sick of me in their jails!!

This was going to be it, after eighteen years of war! And that's all it was with me, a fucking war. I don't believe I won it. I never won fuck all; all I got was a name: 'Britain's most dangerous con', big deal! What forty-year-old man wants that label? I never set out to be who I am, no more than the Krays did. No more than anybody did. It just happens; it's fate, it's meant to be!

That said, perhaps in a sense I did win: I was getting out, after all.

We are what we are – accept it! I accepted that I'm unacceptable! Now it was time to change! To start fresh. New Brighton was my destination – yippee!

CHAPTER 7

RATS AND FACES

It was while I was in Long Lartin that I met the infamous Scottish ex-underworld figure of Jimmy Boyle. The twins always spoke highly of him. Back in the very early 1990s, Jimmy was free – in fact, he had been free for years. There was a forum being televised in the jail, and Jimmy had very kindly consented to come in and take part. It was organised by Johnny Bowden, Danny Foy and several other cons.

I was actually in the seg unit on punishment at the time, for smashing up the TV rooms and assaulting screws. The Governor, Joe Whitty, was asked by Danny Foy if I could come in on the forum. The Governor asked me to give my word that I would behave, so I did and I was allowed in on it. I was asked to describe my feelings on long-time solitary confinement, and how I felt when I was released from Gartree as a Cat A.

The issue was, how can a Cat A – someone, after all, who is considered a danger to the public – be released straight out into the free world? (As I had been, in fact!) They asked me to express myself, and I did! I basically told them it was 'insanity … the system needs a lobotomy!' The forum went out on some TV channel and my bit really hit home; it opened people's eyes. I believe that I did pay a little too much attention to the buffet table that was laid on, but hey, a man's gotta eat something a little more substantial than prison swill.

Jimmy Boyle spoke up well about his life in jail. We all respected it, and he came over brilliantly! It was no secret that Jim had suffered for fifteen years on his life sentence, for a murder he says that he never did. But he made it, got out and did well for himself! Apart from being a gifted sculptor, he's now an award-winning writer. I had a nice chat with him and found him to be everything and more that the twins told me he was – a gentleman, in fact. But with all the notoriety and fame came heartache. In a bizarre twist of fate, Jimmy's son ended up getting stabbed to death in the same street that the person Jimmy was alleged to have murdered died in years before!

At that time, I had served six months less than Jimmy. Now, I've served thirty years, all but a couple of months … I'm now serving life – who the fuck have I killed? My sentence is barbaric.

I'd say to Jimmy, 'Carry on, as you do, keep winning!' It's men like him who help guys like us go on;

it gives the hopeless cases hope! 'Cos there were few like Jimmy in his day. Cages, brutality ... read his book *Sense of Freedom*. That man suffered years of abuse and violence. They made Jimmy Boyle, created him and, once they created him, they could not control him! Once, when Jimmy was on the run, the twins looked after him! Respect!

* * * * *

At this point, I'd like to put a few things straight – there's a lot of actors in the criminal fraternity, but, as time goes by, you get to see their true colours. I'm going to open up a can of worms! The Kray Firm was not all you think they were! The twins, Charlie, Freddie Foreman and Ian Barrie were all solid, bulletproof friends who would die for you. But the rest!

Let's take the Lambrianous, Chris and Tony. They were supposed to be part of the Firm, 'tough guys', men of steel! Call it what you will, they were present the night Reggie stabbed to death Jack the Hat and they got life as well. But did you know Tony ran upstairs and shut himself in a room? Chris sat on the stairs crying – it's a fact. The American mobsters would piss themselves laughing at that!

Fair play, at the trial, they kept silent but, as soon as they got their life sentences, they made statements for their appeal. Both of them blamed the twins; both of them said they were scared; both of them crumbled!

The late Tony wrote his books and went on about how he was a great pal of the twins – well, how could he have been, he made a statement! That statement helped keep the twins in for over thirty years! And guess what? The Lambrianou brothers lost their appeal. So they made their muggy statements for fuck all!

They served their fifteen years and got out – and both of them stayed out. But they are faceless, they're not all you believe them to be. Their statements are public, in books – they can't, or don't, deny them. But they said that their statement was after the trial, that they kept silent for the trial!' Well, I say, a statement is a statement! They made it to win their appeal. It was like saying, 'Fuck the twins, who cares if they serve thirty years!' And it's no joke; it seriously harmed the twins' chances of ever being freed. In my opinion, The Lambrianous are two brothers that can't be respected, but somehow people still see them as big shots! Chris, he found Jesus in prison – so be careful, as he is now in a bigger firm! But, at the end of the day, he would turn against Jesus for his freedom, as he did on the twins!

Ronnie Bender was another one who made statements against the twins after the trial, to win his appeal. His statement was like that of the Lambrianous. The same old shit. Well, the twins fucked him off in Parkhurst! One day, Bender climbed up on the church roof! He shouted over to the twins, 'What's up? Why blank me?' Ron shouted back from his cell window, "Cos you're a rat.' (They had seen his statement for his appeal.)

Then there were the grasses at the trial. Lesley Payne, their own cousin. Scotch Jack Dickson. They both went wrong! Dickson even wrote a book – the fucking cheek of it! No shame! He helps put them away for over thirty years, and then he writes a book about the good old days! And people buy it!

Lets get real: a grass is a grass. You're not half a grass if you put people away, you're a wrong 'un! If you help keep people inside, you're just as bad! A statement is a statement! So why make excuses for people? I'd rather stay in jail than go out on the back of others! In fact, I'd die before I did what the Lambrianous and Bender have done!

Recently, Dave Courtney was slagged off by some old-school villains. Joe Pyle stood by him, and it all turned out to be shit as usual. Dave just gets plenty of 'not guilty' verdicts. He walks, fights it and wins! But some people are jealous of him; I mean, jealous of how he walks. 'Why doesn't Dave Courtney ever get big bird? He must be a wrong 'un!'

Well, I'd say he doesn't get big bird 'cos he's too smart! It's not clever to do big bird ... or is it? Maybe you're not one of the chaps unless you've served twenty years! In that case, best not to be one of the chaps, I'd say! But I'll tell you this: if Dave Courtney went down for twenty years, he wouldn't make a statement to get out and keep some poor cunt in! The likes of Dave are condemned without reason to condemn. The likes of the Lambrianou brothers are held aloft and not condemned, though there's reason to condemn them – get real!

Two of the best armed robbers to come out of London are Bertie Smalls and Don Barrett. Nobody will deny that. Fearless and big-money grabbers. But when it came on top ... they turned supergrass.

Between them, the pair of scum, they helped clean the streets of good men! They destroyed families, put them away for untold years, all to help themselves get off or just get a small sentence.

Johnny Ash – shot dead over a grass. Ronnie Easterbrook – got a life sentence. It happens all the time, people get set up and people get blown away!

So be warned! You don't know what a person's truly like until you see them under pressure! Some scream, some cry, some pick up a pen and make a statement! But a good man will take it on the chin ... ride it! Keep his dignity, never beg, and never crawl. There is still hope, no matter how bleak it gets! But ask yourself this: do you really want to walk free on somebody else's suffering? 'Cos every day you look in the mirror; you'll see a slippery yellow snake looking back at you! The twins' real pals will always know who's who, and what really went down! It's never forgotten!

Another example. While Ron was in Broadmoor, one long-term pal of his was Charlie Smith. Charlie got life in the early 1980s for killing a tramp. Then, he killed his cellmate in the Scrubs and got nutted off! He was only 22 when he arrived at Broadmoor; Ron took a fancy to him. But even he was a joke! Recently I found out the truth about the rat: he got moved to a less secure place and escaped; while he was out he sexually assaulted a woman, now he's back in Broadmoor! So that's the strength of him, he wasn't fit to clean Ron's toilet! And I even gave him a mention in my book *Legends*! So he wasn't what he made himself out to be either!

The twins had the parasites round them for their entire sentence. Maggots chewing off them; maggots that haven't the arse to do anything themselves! They're nothing but fraudsters, actors! But they will all get exposed with time!

Not everyone's like that, of course. One of the twins' most loyal friends was Laurie O'Leary; he visited them for years, right till the end. They admired that man! He did so much for them.

Harry Marsden is another who is the total opposite of what these maggots are all about. Harry is a man of deep pride; he was a good robber, but a gang member did the dirty on him. Harry could have squealed and cut himself a deal, but he never did. Twice, the same gang member ratted on Harry. No one knew who this rat was … and then it came out! Apparently the rat hasn't been seen around for some years. Harry did a lot of bird, but he never squealed on anyone – a good original underworld legend.

Don't do it – be a man! Be like Joe Pyle. Joe wrote a poem about Ron, and Kate Kray put it in her book *Free at Last*. I'm putting it in this book too, as it's brill!

Joe's not a poet – more a philosopher. He wrote this in his cell in max-secure Belmarsh when he wasn't able to get to Ron's funeral. Please, read it slowly, it says it all.

The time has come to say my farewell
But there are a few things I'd like to tell
For twenty-six years they've kept me confined
They said I was mad and out of my mind
I never let my pals down and I never went
to the grain.

* * * * *

I've been what I am, who I am, all I've seen and had, but I still don't consider myself as a face or one of the chaps. After nearly thirty years of being banged up in max secure, with still more to years to survive, I'm still not – nor ever will be – special. I get sack-loads of mail from fans and well-wishers. I've got a club and a website, but I am still just me, not an act! If I have to serve another thirty years, I will, but I'll still only be me. Never see me as what the Krays were, because I'm not – nor do I wish to be. But I'll tell you what: I am a man of my own destiny. As you age, you learn – we all do. Even the insane know what's mad!

CHAPTER 8

FUNERAL FOR
A FRIEND

So my new life began, it wasn't exactly the Costa del Sol, but it was freedom! There are a nice breed of people up that way – friendly and they love a laugh. I used the local gym and the local pool; my fitness was still second to none.

My job on the door was sweet. I worked with Badger, a top-class guy, well respected! Badger was an ex-birdman, so we had a lot in common! But I was fucking lost to life outside; time had passed me by and the kids on the streets had now become 'drug mugs'. I was forever catching the little pricks in the club jacking up! It was a sad reflection of how life was then, in 1992, and it was a fucking disgrace!

I just see drug mugs as a waste of space. A disease! I'd gas the lot of them; send them to Belsen for a cosy weekend in the shower room, as they're no fucking good! They rob off their own family to buy a fix; they would sell their arse for a fix; what good are they to anybody? They're scumbags! Evil little rats! I don't trust them; they make me itch, they're a fucking rash on society! Keep away!

I caught one in the toilet with a needle in his arm, he was out of it, and the kid was no more than eighteen years old, if that! I looked at him and just felt sick. I picked him up, put him over my shoulder and carried him out through the packed club and outside into the cold air. I sat him up against the wall of the car park and three of his pals came out of the woodwork!

I said, 'Why don't you slags take him home!'

One of them got lippy, so I smacked him, then I made it clear to them: 'Don't ever step in my face again 'cos I'll weigh you in!' (I'd weigh half the planet in if it fucked with me!) 'Go on, fuck off, the lot of you!'

One stayed back and we had a chat. I think I got through to him. It felt good to think that I may have saved somebody from a life of shit.

I was walking back to my flat one night, when a car came at me. Luckily I was fast and dived out the way, but there's no doubt it was a deliberate act on my life. I love it when the heat is up high, though, I come alive! 'Come and get me,' that's my way. 'Come out of your holes and get me!'

I would pop over to Liverpool from time to time and see some friends, ex-birdmen, sort some biz out. I'd go up to Leeds to see my old pals Brian Ismund, Ed Clinton and Ed Holland. It was so good to be free!

I sent the twins a parcel each. I got Reggie a nice tracksuit and trainers and I got Ronnie a silk tie and cufflinks, just to let them know I was thinking of them and returning the favour of what they had done for me! I used to look up at the stars at night as I walked in the night air, and I'd think how Ron and Reg would love to do this, and how people just do not realise what freedom is all about. The twins had now spent 23 years inside, 23 fucking years! Dirty paedophiles don't serve half of that! All of the IRA never served that long! It's a disgrace! Reg phoned and said he was made up with his tracksuit. I told him I was gonna do some more fights and he wished me well!

Then all hell fell in on me. I hit a geezer – one punch (he deserved it!) – and I broke his nose. Crack! Next day, armed cops swarmed all over me and I was arrested! And, get this, I was charged with GBH, firearms and conspiracy to rob a bank in Harpenden with persons unknown! Don't make me fucking laugh! Rob a bank? What fucking bank and who with? It was a blatant fit-up! Yes, I broke this geezer's nose, guilty, but I only hit him once. He had been abusive and had been bashing a woman up. I was now in trouble – big fucking trouble!

I told the magistrate, 'Look, I'm innocent of all the charges except the assault!' But I was remanded back into custody and transported to Woodhill Jail, in Bedfordshire. On arrival, they put me straight into solitary. The governor, at the time, Bridie Clarke, told me, 'For as long as you are in my jail, you will be kept in the block!'

I was sick, gutted! Some of my family came in to see me. I told them, 'Believe me, I never did it, there was no bank job, I didn't have a gun!' All in all, it turned out to be a sick plot by somebody we know! A 'she'! And she made a statement! The gun was her gun! A silly starting pistol! It was ridiculous, but it was looking naughty for me. I had only been free for five weeks. I was trying to sort my life out. I did not need this shit!

After four weeks of Woodhill, I felt like it had been four years. Time was dragging. Then something happened: I went to court and all the charges were dropped – well, all except for the charge for the broken nose.

I said, 'Look, you've had me in jail for four weeks for something I told you I did not do. You know it was not my gun. It's destroyed my chances of changing. Yes, I broke a nose, for that you can punish me, but do I need prison? Do I?'

I got a big fine and was told to pay compensation!

'British justice,' I shouted, 'is the best in the world!' (I couldn't get out of that court fast enough.) I shot up back to New Brighton! Fuck me, it was close, a close call – too fucking close! I was so lucky! And the truth was, I had been innocent! Now I knew how it felt. If it had turned out nasty, I believe I would have died in jail – they would have had to kill me. I couldn't serve time for fuck all!

The twins both sent me cards and, again, wished me

well! Ron wrote, 'You've more jam than Hartley's.' Reg told me to use my luck in a positive way!

* * * * *

It felt to me as though my luck was changing. I made a few calls down to London to sort a fight out and told Paul, my manager, that I wanted a good ten grand. He said, 'Leave it to me.'

Life was looking up, my door work and a few deals here and there, I got into a bit of money collecting, and yeah, I was sweet.

Then I got this call! And, like a cunt, I listened! It was a bit of work! Everything laid on, shooter, car, the works. I'm on the way, I was buzzing! (Look, I'm a villain; it's in my blood.) Some people enjoy smoking, drinking, sweets or sex. I enjoy a bit of work – it's in me, I love it, it's my buzz! I could not change! (And I tried! Look what had just happened: I got set up! What's to say I won't get set up again? Life's a gamble; I'm a gambler. I'm a man and I make the decisions. I was on it!

A man called Paul Lucas ran the local garage. He was also running the guns and had been for some time, but what nobody knew was that it was a front. He was, in fact, hunting for the pigs! He was a friend of some friends and they put him my way!

The job I was on was another set-up, but this time Bronson was dead. It was all planned to have me shot.

We had the best driver in Bedfordshire. I had the

shotgun, I was doing the bit of work, and we were set! It was going to be a lovely bit of work. On the day, we were outside the bank in Luton, all was sweet: my bally (balaclava) was on ready to come down over my face; gloves on; extra shells. I was ready!

Then, crash! It was like *The Sweeney*, we had a dozen armed cops in our face! If I blinked we were both dead ducks!

I was remanded to Woodhill. That was one week after I had escaped the last fit-up. Now I was in trouble! Prison was now my life! There was no escape! I got sent down, but my sentence never mattered as, more than ever, I was now on a mission of madness! I had lost my fucking mind! My soul was ablaze; all I wanted was to kick some arse! I was on a one-way ride to hell. Fuck Felix, fuck Lucas; I was on my own mission! (Pray they never enter it.)

Soon after, Paul Lucas ended up in court. But he done deals. He was a supergrass; he got a pathetic sentence and served it in Reading's protection wing. But what the judges and pigs don't realise is that without cunts like Lucas there would be less villains, as it's the likes of Lucas who puts the guns our way! We can't do the job without the guns, so why not give him thirty years?

The twins were gutted for me; my family were devastated. Me, I felt like I had let the whole planet down! My freedom had been only a matter of weeks this time, less than in 1987. It was now January 1993, I had been freed on 14 November 1992, and that was it for me: 41 years old, my vision, my future was prison. Somebody had to pay for it. God, someone would! And that's how it all started: Woodhill – hostage (staff); Belmarsh – hostage (three Iraqis); Bullingdon – hostage (solicitor); Hull – hostage (governor); Hull – hostage (teacher); Winson Green – hostage (doctor).

Now it's 2004 and I'm still Britain's most dangerous con! So let me go back to 1993 and tell you how I kept losing the plot! It's not that I woke up and said to myself, 'Right, I'm on a hostage buzz.' It doesn't happen like that. You can't plan it like that in a prison block. My world is 23 hours a day behind a closed door, so you don't get the opportunities to plan it! It just happens – one split second and it's on! Smash! And that's how it is with me.

My life became a forever journey again, block to block, cage to cage, one solitary cell to the next. When their guard dropped, I was in like a buzzard. I spent a long time up in that special cage in Wakefield known as the Hannibal Suite. Life became one big black hole. It was while I was in the cage that I took up art! Today I love to create. I also took up poetry and writing, I now have seven books and a video to my name: 1/ *Birdman Opens His Mind*; 2/ *Silent Scream*; 3/ *Bronson*; 4/ *Legends*; 5/ *Solitary Fitness*; 6/ *Bronson's Good Prison Guide*; 7/ *The Krays and Me* and (Video): *Sincerely Yours*. Not bad for an ex-Broadmoor madman, eh? I kept up my cell workouts; my press-ups are still second to nobody.

* * * * *

Reg surprised us all by getting married to Roberta, that was some wedding. Reg stated that Maidstone town would be lit up with fireworks, and that's what happened – the sky lit up! Reg could watch it from his cell! Maidstone had never seen fuck all like that before, it was brilliant!

I've never met Roberta. Never likely to meet her as she is just a plain woman, a teacher, a really educated woman, from a good family. Why or how she came into Reg's world is beyond me, but he loved her. After so long in jail, nobody could really have been against Reg being happy, and Roberta made him happy, so it had to be a good thing.

Lots of people said he only did it for parole, but let's get it right: Reg never did anything for parole. He would not even say he was sorry for killing Jack the Hat. (Often, he was asked if he regretted it. He always said, 'Why should I be sorry!') Jack McVitie was a very dangerous man, and he was a fucking hard man; he was scared of nobody. When he had a drink in him, he was everybody's nightmare! He had pulled a gun out and said he would kill the twins; he had also nicked money that had belonged to them – he was mugging them off, so what does anybody do when a lunatic says, 'I'll blow you away,' do you wait for it to happen? You've two choices: report it or act on it! The twins dealt with things in their own way, that's the men they were. Others kill people, get as little as ten years and get out! So why was Reg still in after 31 years?

Ronnie was a different kettle of fish! When you're certified insane, it's up to the doctors when you get out, not the courts!

Personally, I believe Reg was a political prisoner. They had to keep him in as a trophy on show to the rest of the criminal world, as if to say: 'Behave yourselves otherwise you'll end up in the trophy room.' Look at what happened to Ronnie Biggs – there wasn't a home secretary who had big enough balls to let him out!

The twins had too many people in their pockets – some from high-up places: lords, MPs and all sorts. They pulled more strings than a puppet show, believe me!

* * * * *

During the course of my jail term, I copped more years over the Woodhill and Hull siege! My sentence was now fifteen years, but it just made me worse. I was just out of control; I saw no end to it! Death would have been a blessing! I actually asked to be shot, while I had the governor hostage up in Hull. 'Shoot me. Waste me,' I told him. And I meant it.

Then something happened that sent me into a deep hole. My dad died ... that was like an axe in my head! I felt cold and empty. I never realised just how much I loved him till he died. Death is never easy to accept; it's even harder when you're not there for them. Looking back, I feel my dad needed me; I was not there for him, that's what hurts. The day after his cremation, I was

almost kicked to death – the screws in the Scrubs done me in good and proper, as they thought I was out to do them. They feared what I might do, so they did it first! All I wanted was to be left alone and to grieve in my own way. It was a sad fucking time, and I was at my lowest ebb. The same mob of cowards all got nicked later for assaults on other cons, but what about me? Fuck all happened in the way of prosecutions over the assaults against me!

My world began to shrink; I went deep inside myself for some time, depression set in, bouts of anxiety. Then Ronnie died. That day shattered me! The cunts even nicked his brain (without permission). It was only when Kate noticed something was strange about his body that the alarm bells were raised. It was put back after a stink!

RON'S FUNERAL

Well, you all seen it. Fit for a king. It was the biggest funeral before Lady Di passed away … awesome! (If you've forgotten it, then you're a muppet.) It was brill. It was one of the proudest days of my life. That said it all to me!

My pal Dave Courtney sorted that funeral out, and no better man could have done it! It was magic! Everybody from tramps to lords turned up to show their respects. They all loved the Colonel! Did you see that crowd? The procession, that was Ronnie Kray … the man himself!

London came to a standstill. Members of my family represented me; they rode in the procession in a limo I hired. They were there for me, all my friends went there, half the country went, the other half watched it on TV. The planet watched it! Not me, though: I was in solitary. In fact, I forget what a TV looks like! But I was there in spirit. My heart and soul were there that day.

At the service, they played 'My Way'. It was brilliant!

Kate took it bad. But she's a fighter! She's got her head sorted and carried on writing books. Now she's remarried and has found happiness. Who said blondes were dumb? Kate's a winner; she was born to win and she always will!

I saw the press the next day; the grief on Reggie and Charlie's faces. Charlie looked old, worn out! Reggie looked lost! Ronnie's best pal, Joey Pyle, was in a max-secure cell, and he could not be there either. Me and him were gutted not to be there. Ron was only 61 years old when he died. His pallbearers were brother Charlie, Freddie Foreman, Teddy Dennis and Johnny Walsh – men of respect.

Without Ron, it would never be the same. Reg was still in Maidstone, his two pals of old were there for him, Joey Martin and Freddie Foreman, and they helped him through it, but imagine how Reg was! Try to imagine it! How he got over it is beyond me. In fact, did he ever do it? Did he ever get over such a loss? It seemed to me that Reg was never the same again; half of him died along with Ron, and it was now just an empty struggle! No more letters to Ron, no more visits, no more phone calls. Ron was gone.

Me, I'd miss him a lot – his advice, his humour, his letters and his true friendship. For over twenty years, he had stood in my corner, always there for me; he was like a dad to me! I did try to see Ron when I was out, but Broadmoor said 'No'! I also planned to see Reg as soon as he had a spare V/O (visiting order) for me. It wasn't to be! Fuck all ever seems to work out the way you want it to!

An old friend of the twins, Jack Lee – someone who was very close to Ron – said it all when Ron died: 'There will never be another.'

* * * * *

It was a sad time, but you have to go on – you must, you have to! Night turns to day, it's life and we all have to face the end. After Ron's death, life carried on for me. Things were madder than ever, if anything! For starters, I grabbed some Iraqis hostage in Belmarsh! It cost me another seven years – now I was serving 22 fucking years! The British Army was giving away medals to its soldiers for fighting the Iraqis! Me, I got seven years. Madness! It was a really shit time!

Then I took a solicitor hostage, then a doctor! I had just given up any hope of ever getting out! My life was a 'lifemare'! My world was a box! Total isolation!

Then my granny died – more pain! Yeah, she was

getting on a bit, but so what? I wasn't there for her either. That's what hurt the most; it's pain on pain.

And it looked like more bad news was on the way. Dave Courtney was up in the Old Bailey, charged with a whole bundle of fitted-up things ... but Dave walked! I've never known anybody walk out of trials like Dodgy Dave Courtney. Smart fella. But Charlie Kray was not so lucky – he got twelve years, twelve fucking years, at his age, it was really a disgrace! Charlie took it bad! The slags moved him right up north to Frankland! Why? 'Cos he was Charlie Kray.

Charlie took bad, and later he got moved to Parkhurst. He seemed to be getting on with it ... then it happened. Charlie was moved to St Mary's Hospital in Newport – just over the road from Parkhurst. He was in the same room, the same bed I was in when I had been stabbed up. Reggie was in Wayland Jail, but they moved him (under heavy escort) to Parkhurst, so he could see Charlie.

Charlie died in St Mary's. The judge who had given Charlie the twelve years had given Charlie a death sentence – and he was innocent!

Reg was in Charlie's cell. Imagine it: all of Charlie's photos, letters and bits and pieces. Reg was in there before and after he died. Try to imagine the pain Reg was suffering! Thirty-one fucking years he had now served! He had lost everybody and now he was sitting in Charlie's cell, alone. He could smell Charlie in his cell, in a jail Reg had spent eighteen years in.

Reg now had to dig deep, deeper than even before. He was now at the crossroads! He had lost it all; all he had now was Roberta and his close friends! His mind must have been in agony! Was he next to die? Would he ever be freed? What had he done to be in so long! Imagine that man's pain, the tears he shed, the sadness! What a brave man to handle all that grief!

Charlie's funeral was what you expect for a great guy – the best. They all turned out for it – the best for the best! Reg was cuffed up as usual – just like at Ron's funeral and his beloved mother's; chained up like a dog!

Reg went back to Wayland Jail to get on with his life, like the man he was! But was he the same man? Would you be? Could anybody be? Most men couldn't survive thirty days of Reggie's life, let alone thirty years! This is no ordinary man we're talking about. This is an icon!

Reggie's letters became fewer and fewer. I gave it time – time is the healer! I hoped Roberta would keep him up.

One bright spot on my horizon was that Kate Kray started to visit me. I think if you ask her she would say that Whitemoor was the worst visit. At the time, I was on a ten-guard riot unlock, shields, the lot. They intimidated Kate, her face said it all: she hated it! 'Cos she is not a woman to be messed with! She will tell you the same, she hated that hellhole.

I've had that for thirty years: shields in my face, evil tension and paranoia and over-the-top screws! Most of it, I admit, I brought upon myself. I'm not crying – what is there to cry about? Throw me in a pit of snakes and I'll get used to it; whip me and I'll enjoy it! A man can get used to anything after a while. It doesn't mean F.A.

So would Reg make it out? Would all his fight give in? I think we all knew deep down in the end! After 33 years, Reg lost his fight to the big 'C', a battle he could not win! He wasted away, it killed him – and the Home Secretary freed him only weeks before he died!

He won his freedom. He died free, without screws in his face, without a number for his name! He died with friends around his bed, men he admired, Joey Pyle, Fred Foreman, Johnny Nash and, of course, Roberta, who had been with him all through his illness. Reggie's wish was for his pals of old to carry his coffin. That was his wish, his dying wish! But, on the day, it was not respected. Roberta said no to it, and the people carrying the coffin should never have done it and it saddened a lot of people. Some people were so disgusted at it that they didn't even turn up.

The pallbearers had not even known Reg for ten years between them all! How could they push men like Joe Pyle out? Men who had known Reg all their lives! Joe, Fred and Johnny had not only known Reg, they had fought with him, bled with him, cried with him, won with him and lost with him! Those carrying the coffin were prats, it had to be said! Would they have kept their mouths shut like Freddie Foreman did? Fred served ten years of his life for the twins' honour!

Men like Joe Pyle are a dying breed. One of those

pallbearers was a shit fucking pop singer – what right did he have doing that? That was Reg Kray, 'The Man', 'The Survivor', 'The born fighter'! It should have been his life-long pals! Men he loved and respected, men he trusted. Believe it, it was a disgrace!

Ronnie Kray would have screamed in his grave! And Reggie would not have been happy! Face facts, Reg was a villain, proud of it. He had no regrets, he done what he done!

The turnout was brilliant – all walks of life turned up. It wasn't half what Ron's was but, like I said before, Ron was special. I believe Roberta made a big mistake that day, but it's done. We all have to get on with our lives.

CHAPTER 9

SELLING OUT

On 14 July 1997, Ron married Roberta at Maidstone Jail. Like all notorious weddings, it attracted great interest in the media – and most felt it to be a circus. Basically it was a fucking joke to the media. But, little do they realise, it's people's lives.

Feelings run even more strongly if you're inside, whether you are Reg Kray or the Count of Monte Cristo. You don't need problems on the big day. On the eve, Reg had arranged for a massive laser show up in the sky. Something Maidstone would never forget, it was awesome and all the lads could see it from their cell windows. I have met cons that were there and all said it was brilliant. Only Reg could have sorted such a spectacular event. Reg even got into trouble over it. As always, the system hated anything that's creative or that makes people happy. Is it out of jealousy? How the fuck can anybody be jealous of a man who's been locked up for thirty years, but they are. You all saw the twins at their mum's farewell. You all saw Reg at Ron's farewell; you saw the crowds, the massive support. That is why they were so despised by the system – because they were so loved by their own people.

So on 14 July 1997, the circus took off, the games started up. Maidstone Jail attempted to spoil the party, to spoil the big day, by not allowing photos of the big wedding. They just sprang it on Reg. They would be taking photos, but they would be Crown copyright and Reg and Roberta would have to sign over all the rights to to them, or they wouldn't get the photos. It took fifteen months before Roberta got them. Can you believe this shit?

And guess who was best man? Yes, the biggest clown of all, Bradley Allardyce. A traitor, a total and utter toe rag. He sold Reg out in death. You've got a lot to live with, Bradley. Every day you are awake, I bet it is on your mind. It sure should be, because what you did to Reg will haunt you until you are gone. Even Roberta must despise you. I know all the chaps do. I had best clear it up now, as I know you are all in suspense.

Bradley Allardyce was the rat that secretly photographed Reg on his bed when he was dying and sold the photo to the press. That was the photo you all see of Reg in bed, with tubes out of his body looking like death.

At first, poor old Wilf Pine was blamed, he was even

pulled over it, and Wilf was an old-time pal. A dignified man, with morals and respect and he was blamed over it. And all the time it was that toe rag. Reggie's best man.

How could a man like Reg have such a dog as best man? It is beyond me, I could never understand it. Ronnie would have gone mad over it. Joe Pyle was Ron's best man; ask anybody who was Reggie's and they all laugh. Because it is a fucking joke. He couldn't be best man for Charles Manson, let alone our Reg.

One good thing about the day was that Reg and Roberta could cut their wedding cake; at my own wedding I was denied a knife. We were also denied the photos and my wife lost the case for use of our wedding photos in a proposed book. And the crazy thing is Ken Blackman, my best man, turned out to be a toe rag as well!

Personally, I was happy for Reg, because, after being alone for so long, to have somebody that truly loved him was a special gift of life. I doubt anybody could or would say that Roberta did not love Reg. I guess she suited him. I thought they were good for each other, but, in the end she changed Reggie's true identity.

Love can be blind. Reg lost the plot with it. And his death just a few short years later became a circus, a joke. Look at the pallbearers: Allardyce and three other nobodies. It should have been the men who really loved him, men who fought alongside him, friends of fifty years, not five-minute mugs. It upset a lot of people, it caused a lot of bad feelings, for me included.

Reg was a legend, and no disrespect to Roberta, but she could never realise or understand the whole sadness this funeral caused.

Roberta is a lovely lady who worshipped Reg, but the end was a fucking joke. She will be the first to admit that Allardyce disrespected Reg and sold him out; he even did stories about Reg after the funeral alleging that he was Reg's lover. And he admitted he took the photo of Reg in hospital – what more proof do you need? But he still carried Reggie's coffin, that to me is an insult to a great man. I think of men like Joe Pyle, John Nash, Fred Foreman, Roy Shaw, Ian Barrie: did they ever betray Reg or sell him out? Did they fuck.

Reggie's real friends were life-long pals, men of rock. Why allow such a ponce to carry Reg off. I wonder whose tea boy Allardyce is now? What a crazy life this is. One sure thing: I am being cremated; I don't want anybody messing with my end. Mine will be as mad as my life is. Ashes in a pot, up in a chopper, spread over Broadmoor grounds. I am back.

* * * * *

I guess it was always going to be a sad end. It was for Ron, it was for Charlie. So it was destined to be the same for Reg. Nobody could change fate.

Thirty-plus years of jail didn't beat Reg, he survived it all. Could you? Reg's illness was the thing that destroyed him; that cancer was to eat him away.

Memories of Reg. A man of great mental strength. Plenty of heart, bottle, a dry sense of humour. For almost thirty years, Reg was a part of my journey through the prison life, and I can honestly say I really felt nothing but good thoughts in Reggie's company. He either liked you or despised you. There was no halfway with Reg, no sitting on the fence shit – come in or get the fuck out.

I still meet cons on my travels who did a bit of time with him. Recently, in Whitemoor seg unit, I met a young guy called Danny Marcovitch, 26 years old, who met Reg. He was telling me how well Reg got on there and he was well liked by all, even the screws treated him with respect.

Reg was a great one for inventing things. I remember one of his creations in particular: a table tennis ball on a string hanging from the light in his cell. He would use it for his boxing skills. Just a flick of the ball and away he went, his head rolling and bobbing, weaving, all for speed. People forget Reg spent nearly eighteen years in Parkhurst. Nearly eighteen fucking years in one jail.

While Ron had a lot of luxury in the asylum, Reg had just the basics of life: a radio, a piss pot and lots of security, forever on Cat A.

It took Reg twenty years to come off Cat A. He was a very fit man, he took a lot of pride in his fitness; life for him was a routine. He made self-discipline work for him; he would put everything into a project and not stop until he finished it. He created his first book in

Parkhurst in the 1980s: *Cockney Rhyming Slang*. It wasn't a masterpiece, but it was a great achievement, and from that many more projects followed. I think that the best was *Born Fighter*, which he wrote in Gartree in 1987.

He was also a good poet and a man of philosophical intellect. As for art, although his works sell for plenty, he couldn't paint for toffee. But a Kray painting is a collector's item, whatever it is. And most of the money went to charities. Reg had a big heart for helping kids; he also did a lot for boxing clubs such as Repton's in Bethnal Green.

People forget all this – or is it that they don't want to know? I think it is that they don't want to believe. Well, they had better start believing it, because it is all true. Robin Hood was a diamond too; criminals aren't all bad. Wake up and smell the coffee.

* * * * *

Two days before Ron died, I sent Reg a book called *Positive Thinking*. It's a powerful book. I don't know why I sent it when I did. I signed it to both Ron and Reg, but I sent it to Reg – maybe it was fate, to help him be strong.

As for myself, I would like to do something positive, as I want Ron to be proud of me. He wanted me to be free and happy, as I also wanted him to be. I wanted so much to see the twins go free, if our system wasn't so cruel and pig headed, they could have lived as free men years ago.

This concrete coffin that closes up and wraps a stone wall around us makes it difficult to express our true selves. We get labelled and branded and we have to live with it. Years pass by, we get older, wiser, but the label still sticks.

My madness goes on. I always thought that I would end up back in Broadmoor, as it's like a giant magnet dragging me back. Maybe I should go back, just to walk into Ron's old cell and make sure for myself that he is free – totally free, as I truly believe he is. I sense that his death was a blessing – maybe it was his final good deed to Reggie. I'm positive I'll catch up with Ronnie, Reggie and Charlie in the next world, God Bless you all, forever in my heart.

As for me, I plod on. I've lost too much, and don't ever intend to let this concrete coffin blow out my light.

CHAPTER 10

THE THOUGHTS
OF REG KRAY

Everyone kicked up a big fuss when the Alder Hey Hospital in Liverpool snatched dead children's body parts without so much as asking for the parents' permission to do so. So why, then, when the Home Office snatched the brain of the dead Ronnie Kray, could they get away with it without a word being said? Why did they take his brain for examination? They will have wanted to see what a big-time gangster's brain looked like: weighing it, measuring it, photographing it, dissecting it. Eventually, the brain was returned, but not before Reggie had kicked up a fuss.

In my opinion, you will not find out what makes a man tick by taking out his brain, cutting it into small pieces and examining it under a microscope – contrary to what the Home Office believes to be the case! What makes a man tick, what sets man apart from the rest of the creatures on earth? Ask David Attenborough! But I can tell you this: I knew what made *Reggie* Kray tick and, to prove this point, I want to use a piece of him that everyone seems to have overlooked. A really smart piece of Reggie's make-up was his thoughts. Academics study the thoughts of Aristotle, Pythagoras or Freud and come up with their conclusions as to what made these people tick; I too can offer the same with respect to Reggie Kray.

How does one dissect the thoughts of Reg Kray? What way can I trawl the thoughts of such a man and know for certain that what I am looking at is the truth? Easy! Long before true crime books became so popular, Reg had written in his own hand a book that should have been accepted as nothing less than startling! But it wasn't to win any awards and sold very few copies of a short print run.

In my opinion, there is only one book that really explores the mind of Reg Kray, and that is his book *Thoughts: Philosophy & Poetry*. It reveals what really went on in Reg's mind when he was behind bars, just as Joe Pyle's book *Looking at Life* did. Reggie's book was printed as he had written it – without publisher's editing, with textual and grammatical errors that were left in and with no apology for this.

In fact, the write-up that appeared in the book on this particular matter even had a textual error in it (see if you can spot it):

The text is presented to the reader, un-edited by the publisher.

The main text was created over a nine-hour period, which gives and insight into this man's unique mind. Hence, textual and grammatical anomalies remain.

As stated, Reg created the main text for this book over a nine-hour period in 1990 whilst in Lewes Jail. Imagine revealing things about yourself over a nine-hour period! Some people can hardly talk about themselves for nine minutes, let alone nine hours!

The book is a one-off and is very rare to find in the shops. Its original publisher was River First Publishing. I believe it is no longer in print, though if you want to try and look for it, the ISBN number was: 0951818007. The dedication was to: 'My late wife Frances and my son Brad because they both have the same quality of sweet innocence.' Do you really think that if Ron had anything to do with the death of Frances that Reg would have condoned it, especially as he dedicates his book to her with such fervour. And for Reg to use the word 'innocence' ... well, get the picture?

I, too, am a poet – as proven by my bucketload of Koestler Awards for my prose and my book *Birdman Opens His Mind*. Knowing Reg as I did and actually talking about some of these pieces in his book, I can reveal a lot more for you about him, just as Reg does in his book.

The book should have sold a million, but it was read

by philistines, it fell by the wayside and was, largely, ignored as 'just another one of those damn prison poem books'. But, as I mentioned earlier, I believe that this small hardback book revealed more about Reg Kray than any other book I've ever cast my eyes on. So here goes on my dissection of some of his work.

In the book's introduction (which isn't actually called an introduction), Reggie reminisces about courting days – and, by this, he doesn't mean the days he spent at the Old Bailey!

Interestingly, Reg describes himself as being in 'exile', not as being 'imprisoned'. This use of the word 'exile' is a slip-up that reveals a lot more about Reg than would have otherwise been revealed – he clearly always felt, and hoped, that he would be released.

'Yesterday is today's memory, tomorrow is today's dream': an apt quotation from Reg that says it all. What he means by this is that the more you toil, the more you will reap the rewards of that hard work. As fast as Reg was building the Kray Empire, Ron was destroying it. Reg was a builder of dreams; he was the eternal romantic, always living in hope.

'Do you remember talking to your fiancé for hours when you were courting and how you would both dream of your future together and ambitions?' Here, Reggie uses the masculine spelling for 'fiancé' (the feminine spelling is 'fiancée'), but it is believed he meant to use the feminine spelling, as he is directing this thought to the male reader. I know from this that he was talking from his own experiences of the time he spent courting his then fiancée Frances. His dreams along with those of Frances must have seemed a far-off memory when all turned lemon in that relationship.

Reg goes on to write: 'Sometimes as we get older we cease to dream.' This is a clear indication that he is looking within himself when he reveals that, with age, he is dreaming less. 'Do not be deterred, allow yourself to dream': this is a rhetorical command that Reg is putting to himself. He is still, at this time in 1990, pushing himself on, driving forward and being his own taskmaster, still not deterred, at this time, by the twenty-plus years he has spent behind bars.

'I see one's brain and mind as one would see a diamond, with various shapes and glittering effects. I myself have a butterfly mind, which jumps around to and fro all over the place.' This has overtones of Wordsworth's 'I wandered lonely as a cloud'. Here, Reg uses the analogy between a brain and diamond to show what he says is the 'shape of diamond which reflects one's thoughts'. (I wonder if this is where the saying 'diamond geezer' came from?) As Reg continues writing about this, he talks of being burdened with cares and shackled by chains – another indication that Reg is burdened by his own incarceration.

Although Reg goes on to say that his intention is to influence the reader to free themselves of man-made chains, he sees himself as being liberated from incarceration by his ability to be set free by virtue of his 'thoughts' being free: 'Each night I abandon my chains and wander with my thoughts in any direction I wish to choose.'

Reg said that he was born to be violent, and this is consolidated when he says: 'Prior to my arrest I used to feel slighted very easily and would react to a slight with a return of violence. Then I realised that violence usually erupted because of lack of verbal expression.' What Reg is saying, I too have said, but then a black cloud can come over you and 'verbal expression' goes out of the window. Reg has certainly found himself by this stage – instead of resorting to violence, he is beginning to understand the value of words.

'If I sat down with my adversary and out-reasoned them verbally, then violence was not necessary.' Sadly for Reg, this particular gem of a thought was too late in the offing. The violence was over, in the past, but no amount of words was going to wash it away, and he knew it. He was just reinforcing what he had learned over the years of being banged up, which was that talking could solve problems.

Again, Reg mentions the 'diamond of the mind' in helping the reflections to shape our thoughts and promote conversation. In comparison to his brother Ron, Reg was a man apart. He wanted to talk and enjoyed intelligent conversation. Whereas Ron would and could remain quiet for hours and days at a time.

A clue to how Reg wishes to be perceived and to what he is revealing at this stage in his life is when he writes: 'I invite the reader to be analytical on my various thoughts. I do with intention that is for the benefit of my many supporters throughout the country who write to me each day their letters of support, so that they can begin to know me and that we are no longer strangers and so that my thoughts may influence them to be my friends as well as supporters.' Here, Reg is inviting the reader to pick his brain and see what makes him tick.-

Within the book there are a number of poignant poems written by Reg. One in particular offers some tell-tale signs of how he's managing after twenty-plus years behind bars:

20 YEARS IN JAIL

Twenty years in jail
This wasn't part of my goal
Twenty years in time freedom has not been mine
Twenty years I've not seen the sky at night
It's getting tougher for me
When will I be free?
There's just a few more years left
Because the night of my life grows dim
So the end could be in sight
I mean to make it before then
It's been twenty years in jail
They say it's eight to ten more before I'm free
Before the end
But I have Consolation

Because I met a friend
My philosophy is to enjoy the moment
The past is behind
The future too distant
So the moment is mine
I've shared the laughter and tears with my friend
So have no fears
My friend has given me a happy heart
Even if the night draws near
So how can I regret?
There's many less fortunate
I may make it beyond the gate yet
To once again see the night
So let's not regret
And let now be the moment
Because it's close to the night.

Taking Reg at his word to be analytical, I will be. Reg is crying out to be heard, and he's able to put into words what he wasn't willing to do. Although Reg and Ron wouldn't bow down to the system, take responsibility for their crimes and renounce what they had done, within this poem it can be seen that Reg is asking a big question: 'when will I be free'!

An acceptance that Reg is in the middle years of his life can be detected in the line: 'There's just a few more years left.' In an almost pleading way, Reg continues: 'Because the night of my life grows dim.'

Already, someone in authority has been talking to

Reg – he says in his poem: 'They say it's eight to ten more [years] before I'm free.' He accepts that his hoped-for freedom is some way off, yet he lives in constant hope that his name will be pulled out of the hat of hope.

Consolation in his fate is accepted when he is able to refer to a friend who has helped him through: 'I've shared the laughter and tears with my friend.'

Hope is the mainstay of this poem: 'I may make it beyond the gate yet.' And yet despondency also creeps into Reg's thoughts – there's always the possibility that freedom may never come his way: 'I may make it beyond the gate yet.' The key word here is 'may'. A dreamer living with reality.

Although Reg asked when he would be free, he left a lot of the campaigning for his freedom to others. His wife, Roberta, worked to get him out of prison, but she lacked the pizzazz and showmanship needed to get such a bid for freedom off the ground. After all, she was an unknown to the world at large.

ALONE AT NIGHT

Alone at night I stay
And it's the same throughout the day
I've begun to like it this way
I listen to my heartbeat
While most are asleep
And enjoy my thoughts
Of past sorrow and joy
The tears and laughter

All in the silence of the night
While the stars twinkle bright
With my deep thoughts I toy
Past laughter, sorrow and joy
To me silence is golden
To prayer I am beholden
Throughout the night
There's not a stir
An acorn of an idea is my spur
I seek ambitions to fulfil
All the time the night is still
I look to a sense of fulfilment
To an idea that will bring agreement
I am chained physically
But my mind is free
So I wander the night
All targets in sight
My thoughts wander beyond the gate
As to how imprisonment is my fate
Is it too much that one day I'll be free?
It's a day that's difficult to foresee
Especially in the loneliness of the night
Such a day seems way out of sight
Yet, to dream is part of my philosophy
That such a day I will see
To me each moment is mine
A gem of time I do not wish to see go by
So there's no rush to meet my fate
Even if it means beyond the gate

> I try not to fight against the tide
> With each moment I ride
> Each day is a moment of Fate
> So there's no rush to go beyond the gate
> Each day makes me free
> Because of my philosophy
> Is it such a bad fate?

Free, free, free. The word 'free' appears three times in this poem. Gone is the pleading question 'when will I be free', to be replaced with the more poignant line of: 'Is it too much that one day I'll be free?', revealing something of a Dickensian Oliver Twist plea: 'Please, sir ...' There are no demanding words. That was the way of the Krays: no hard one-liners shouted out. In fact, Ron Kray, when miffed at people, would say in a rather gentle but sinister way, 'I'll remember you Mr ...'

Although Reg speaks of freedom, he can't see the day coming. He's in prison, supremely fit and alert, he's everything to live for ... but the world is passing him by! Anyone would get angry if they were in such a position, but Reg, somehow, accepted his fate rather like a cavalry officer. Gone was the working-class hollering, to be replaced by a dignified acceptance of what lay ahead.

As a blade of grass bends with the wind, Reg says, 'I try not to fight against the tide. With each moment I ride.' As if riding a punch in the boxing ring, Reg feels that to go along with the system's demands may well expedite his freedom. But when you look at the likes of most rebellious prisoners (for example, Jimmy Boyle and Jimmy Holland), you see a less strict regime with more carrots of freedom being dangled. With Reg, this was not the case. I sometimes wonder whether Reg might not have attracted more sympathy towards his bid for freedom if he had been a little more rebellious in his ways.

Reg's use of the word 'gem' ties in with his previous explanation of the word 'diamond' to describe the mind. Clearly, Reg is putting a value on time, even if it means time will drag on before his release. You see, for Reg to speed up the time clock of life would have been bad news: he knew his release would be a long way off, but he didn't want to become old before his time, preferring to savour the time he had left.

The metaphorical use for the word 'chained' has been dropped and, here, Reg has used the word 'physically' to tie in the word 'chained': 'I am chained physically'. Reg fought imaginary dragons, much as Don Quixote did. His chains of life had become physical shackles of restriction, which, in his mind, were real. Gone was the fortitude and fire of his fighting days. Here, we see a turning point in Reg's prison life.

When Reg was shipped to Gartree Prison in 1990 (a year before he wrote this particular poem), he found the cons on strike from work protesting about the bad food (unsurprisingly). Here, in Reg's own words, he shows how awkward he feels over the matter: 'When we arrived I was allocated a cell on the second floor. Almost opposite was my old friend Kevin Rusko. He told me that all the cons were on strike from work, protesting about the bad food, and would be refusing to go back to their cells at evening lock-up time. I thought about this and decided that I would compromise by keeping out of my cell for half an hour at lock-up — then I would bang-up. I felt this was showing my solidarity with the cons but at the same time I had to do my own thing. I hadn't had the chance to decide if the food was good, bad or indifferent, and I always like to make my own decisions and not be a sheep.'

While Reg was in Nottingham Prison in 1991, a fellow con had gone berserk and was running riot in the wing office; he was banging a stick on the table and heading for trouble. Reg quelled a possible riot by taking immediate action. He grabbed the con and ran to his own cell with him, banged the door shut and calmed things down. Reg said he did this for the other con, not for himself or for any glory attached to it. He prevented any escalation of violence by getting a screw to come to his cell door and saying that he wanted to escort his fellow con to the block so as to ensure he didn't get a kicking, but that, first, the con wanted to pick his radio up from his cell en route to the block. The screws opened Reg's cell door. All of the wing's cons were standing on the landing and they asked Reg what they should do. One word from Reg and they would have kicked off. Reg told them to stay calm.

So, does this mean that Reg was losing the plot and changing into a right 'governor's boy'? No! From what Reg reveals earlier in his book, he tells us straight, that sitting down and talking can solve things.

Now, I can see where you would be coming from if you said it looked like Reg was prepared to eat shit if it meant he would be freed. But remember this: in order for Reg to start out on the road to freedom all that he had to do was to work on his offending behaviour and start saying sorry. But he didn't. Instead, he kept the Kray legend going. Had the authorities been clever, they would have let the twins out years ago and allowed them to go off into obscurity. Blame the authorities for perpetuating the Kray legend.

In the line 'Each day is a moment of Fate', notice how Reg uses an upper-case 'F' for the spelling of the word 'Fate'. This implies that Reg placed an awful lot of faith in the lap of the gods – he was a chancer.

PUPPY DOG BE MY FRIEND
Puppy dog be my friend
I know you are loyal
And will stay with me till the end
I know I cannot ask for a better friend
Though you cannot speak
Your eyes tell a story that makes me happy
Your soft paw makes me love you all the more
I see the way you watch me move
Your loyalty all the time you prove

Puppy dog, you are my best friend
This is clear to me
Let me give you a hug and a pat
You make me so happy my puppy dog friend
* you do not ask me for a loan
You're content with a bone
You are there early in the morning
When the rest are yawning
You put them all to shame
You are so game
When I say 'let's walk'
Though you cannot talk you know just the same
Each time I call your name
And you walk beside me as my friend

Ronnie was the one to adore animals; he had an Alsatian dog called Freda. So to see Reg give his poem over to a 'puppy dog' may seem odd. Some analysis will reveal a little more insight into Reg's thoughts when he wrote this poem.

The opening three lines of this poem are crucial in revealing a deeper meaning: 'Puppy dog be my friend. I know you are loyal. And will stay with me till the end.' When we look at the amount of people who betrayed the Krays, it is easy to see whom Reg thinks of when he writes this. We've already looked at the grasses and maggots in the lead-up to the end of the Kray era – these are the people he is having a swipe at. Sadly,

* Left in exactly as Reg wrote it

unlike the puppy dog, many of the Kray henchmen never had such loyalty.

The word 'friend' is used in the poem no less than five times, which has a significant meaning to the context Reg applies to this word. All through Reg's life, he had fair-weather friends – there when the sun was shining, gone when the storms loomed overhead! Reg was the last – or, rather, second last – person out of the Kray Firm to realise that his henchmen had betrayed him.

'Let me give you a hug and a pat.' This line seems against all the principles of being a hard man, but is it? Reg wasn't frightened to show his emotions, happy or sad. A hard man can overcome his fears of what people might think of him if he shows compassion, and Reg, indeed, was a man of compassion. Hard to believe about a man who stabbed Jack the Hat in the face and brutally killed him in front of his peers. But when you see the softer side of him – for example, when he spent night after night sitting outside his estranged wife's house talking to her while she sat in the upstairs window – we can then see that Reg was a man of passion. He dearly longed to hug and hold Frances, but he just couldn't combat the demons of the Firm.

'You do not ask me for a loan' – everyone wanted a piece of the Krays, even inside prison. The twins were understated in everything that they did; they had charisma oozing out of every pore in their skin. Who wouldn't want to be a part of their hierarchy? By borrowing from the Krays, you showed your appreciation in many different ways. As much as this amused the twins, it also pissed them off.

'You put them all to shame. You are so game.' Put whom to shame? Many a time, the twins would tell me about the mob that let them down. They told me how certain characters like Freddie Foreman had put the rest of the Firm to shame by being so staunch. Some of you will have heard of the phrase 'He's a game one.' The meaning is simple; you would fight to the end. Reg took great delight in having loyal friends around him, but, if you were a 'game', loyal friend, you surpassed all others.

Reg's definition of a friend was simply this: 'It is said that a man is judged by the company he keeps, so in effect, it is better to have a bed of roses rather than a garden of weeds.' As Reg says, he is not trying to be the teacher to you, the pupil. His book of thoughts is simply a complex translation of mixed thoughts.

I LOST A FRIEND

I lost a friend
And thought it was the end
She was the beginning and the end
Was everything I stood for
When she was near I would ask for no more
But I was never to be with her for the count
of a score
Her life ended all too quickly one sad day
This I did not foresee so it shook me real bad

For a while I was quite mad
How could this happen to us?
To me it was like a curse
When I had been so happy
How could one so young die?
I had to ask the question why
My eyes were dim with tears
We had been like one for years
Now she was gone and not beside me any more
I could not figure the score
Why did this happen to me?
We had been so happy
Now she was no longer there beside me
She was the beginning and now the end.

For those in the know about the Krays, it will be no surprise to learn that this poem refers to the late wife of Reg, Frances. By the time the Firm was arrested, Reg was in a deep depression due to the sad loss of his wife. Suicides are never painless! Reg is at an all-time low when he relates this sad ending for one he wished to spend his life with.

Interestingly enough, Reg writes about a curse in this poem: 'How could this happen to us? To me it was like a curse.' Although the Krays had the Midas touch when it came to building business fortunes, they never had luck when it came to love. Just as Reg explains, it seemed like there was a price to pay for all the success on the business side of things.

As much as Reg wanted to settle down to a family life, the commitments of the Firm came between him and his dream. Ron was the insatiable twin, never being satisfied with what he had, always wanting more but never providing for a rainy day. Reg, on the other hand, looked ahead and wanted the stable life that he could have with Frances. You can't be a gang boss and expect to have a stable family life while running the empire. Reg had heart.

FREE REGGIE KRAY

Free Reggie Kray
He has served his time
Retribution is out of line
Let him have peace at his age
He has paid the wage of his crime
Over twenty years is the gauge of time
And longer is too long
Let this be our song
Free Reggie Kray
He has done his time
Let him out of jail
This is our goal
He has done his sentence
Many years too long
This is our song
Free Reggie Kray
This is what we all say.

As I've already said, the 'Free Reg Kray' mission was poorly supported and, as well as that, poorly administered. Reg was content to play the pacifist in all of this, but he did, at times, make an effort. He was like a sleeping giant – when he erupted, he really erupted!

Interestingly enough, Reg uses the word 'retribution' in this line: 'Retribution is out of line'. Such a word was commonplace to Reg when he was free – anyone dissing him would pay the price. And even more so with Ron. Here, Reg is saying that two retributions don't make a right. The system was using retribution against the twins in a big way. Ron was safely tucked away in Broadmoor, with no fear of ever being freed ... but Reg! Well, he was always the fly in the ointment where the authorities were concerned. By keeping Reg banged up, it was sending an unparalleled message out to all. The longer Reg was banged up, the stronger the message was.

'He has paid the wage of his crime. Over twenty years is the gauge of time': although Reg had been, unofficially, told that he was to serve in excess of his thirty-year tariff, he always hoped the authorities would be wrong. Twenty years in anyone's life is a long, long time. Look at the types of crimes people commit and see how they serve what is considered a just amount of time behind bars for that particular crime. The 'Free Reggie Kray' campaign failed due to a poor marketing strategy. Reg held the key to it all, but he wouldn't put it in the lock.

He has done his sentence. By today's standards, Reg served far in excess of what could be considered a prison sentence commensurate with his crimes, but who cares?

'Free Reggie Kray. This is what we all say.' Who are the 'we' in this particular part of his poem? That was the problem: there were not enough soldiers ... too many maggots feeding off him! Too many 'yes' people surrounded Reg – doesn't that say it all?

In 2000, when Reg was in Wayland Prison, in Norfolk, he was facing another parole review. Reg commented on the negative reports produced by the prison staff: 'I have been in the system far too long to be surprised. I find myself reading yet another set of bizarre and twisted statements, words I have never said.'

Indeed, Reg had done everything and more that was asked of him in his last parole report, yet the parole board wanted him to go on an 'Enhanced Thinking Skills' course. Reg had done everything possible to win parole, everything except jump backwards through hoops of fire, but it still wasn't good enough for them!

Here's a small illustration to show how much Reg was complying with prison authorities and the parole board. Reg was on his way to visit his sick brother, Charlie, in St Mary's Hospital on the Isle of Wight. The van taking Reg there had a 'No Smoking' sign in it. This is what Reg says of it (as before, all spelling and grammar errors have been left uncorrected): 'In March I heard the news that my brother Charlie had been admitted to hospital from Parkhurst. He only stayed a few days before he was returned to prison but continued to feel unwell. I had already put in a request for a visit and when Charlie was readmitted to St Mary's I was told I would be allowed to go and see him.

'I left Wayland at 8am on 18 March with four screws as an escort. One of them was driving the van. As we pulled away from the prison a red Ford car followed us. I thought it was the law but one of the screws told me it was the press. We could see the feller holding a camera. The car followed us all the way to Winchester prison, where we stopped at about 11am. The driver made good time and provided all of us with boiled sweets along the way! There was also a box full of ham and cheese sandwiches, crisps, apples and cartons of milk. Although there were no smoking signs in the van, I was allowed a smoking – which was a relief.'

Anyone who knew the Reg Kray of old would tell you that he wouldn't have complied with any prohibition sign. If there were a sign saying 'Don't piss in the tea urn', then, for sure, he would have done what he was told not to do. Bearing that in mind, look again at the last line of what Reg says: 'Although there were no smoking signs in the van, I was allowed a smoking – which was a relief.' Now here is a man saying how relieved he is to be able to have a smoke 'cos they, the screws, allow him to do so. The big underworld figure of Reg Kray demoted to obeying 'no smoking' signs! Doesn't that tell you how he wanted to be free. And this was ten years after he'd written the poem 'Free Reggie Kray'.

When Reg was diagnosed as being terminally ill, he was, at long last, freed. But! Had Reg been physically fit, he would have been kept behind bars right up until this present time. By dying, Reg did the bastards a favour, and he knew this. When Reg was on his deathbed, he was asked if he felt bitter. He replied that he didn't have the time to feel bitter ... that was Reg.

ON THE RACK

I look around and see
They live off my back
While I dance on the rack
They now have women screws too
All dressed in blue
Prison is an industry
Don't let anyone tell you differently
They keep me in so as to keep them in work
I know this, I'm not a jerk
My life ekes out day by day
But no-one cares of those in charge
As long as I pay their wage
To them I am just their gauge
They are all sworn to secrecy
And don't care one bit about me
Twenty years I have done
And yet another ten to run
They would rather see me dead than alive

As long as they take home the bread
That's why I strive to keep fit
Because one day I'll walk out of that gate
just remember this story I relate
Prison is an industry
Killers, rapists, they integrate
The con's not what he was
the wage is the boss
I'm just a pawn in a game
That's why they continue to shout my name
They'll make sure I do each day
Because I'm Reg Kray
They don't care about me
As long as they are paid to turn the key
They won't like it this way
But I'll have my say
The wage is the name of their game
No they will not like what I have to say
Because my name is Reg Kray.

This poem has to be the ultimate 'look into my head and see my thoughts' poem. If anything could succinctly put across how Reg thought, then this is the one to do it.

'I look around and see. They live off my back.' Here, Reg refers to the screws in the prison system eking out a living from guarding him.

'As long as I pay their wage. To them I am just their gauge.' At the end of a year, a prison officer would be allowed to add an inch of chain to his key chain, so the chain represented how many years he had served as a prison officer. So naturally, a really long key chain meant that a screw had put in a lot of years. Reg refers to himself as being a marker in time so that screws could gauge how long they had served ... just like a key chain being extended by an inch per year.

Reg earned dosh while he was in prison. Ron and him made a good few hundred thousand pounds from the film about their life. Just out of interest, Ray Winstone the actor was originally selected to play both Ron and Reg. (This was to have been done on a split screen.) But in the end the Kemp brothers won the leading roles ... and a nice little earner it was for the twins. I firmly believe that Reg thought he was actually paying taxes from his income to support the Prison Service staff wages.

'They are all sworn to secrecy. And don't care one bit about me.' Reg meant what he said, and he was right. When he was in Norwich Jail, he suffered terribly with acute pain before his cancer was properly diagnosed. One night, Reg suffered so much pain that he pressed his cell 'call' button ... no one responded. What did the screws care! They knew Reg had been in pain with what was at first thought to be Irritable Bowel Syndrome. As it happens, it was full-blown cancer that couldn't be treated.

'That's why I strive to keep fit. Because one day I'll walk out of that gate.' Reg lived for the day he could walk out of prison and say to the world that he was free. By maintaining his fitness in the gym, Reg thought he would live to be a hundred, but the years of drinking prison hooch and his smoking had taken its toll. Nothing wrong with a bit of the old hooch, but sometimes they made it with any old rubbish ... even boot polish. Me, I wouldn't touch the stuff (when I had access to it) unless I knew what it was made from.

'Killers, rapists, they integrate. The con's not what he was the wage is the boss.' Back in 1990, changes within the prison system meant that man management overruled prisoners' conditions. Reg was very perceptive to note this, and what he has said has come true. Now, they know right down to the last farthing how much it will cost to keep a certain category of prisoner locked up. Gone are the days when a prison officer could walk out of prison with a leg of lamb purloined from the prison kitchen.

Nowadays, some prisons integrate kiddy killers and the likes with ordinary cons; it's all down to saving money! Reg could see this happening, and he didn't like it. His school of thought was the old school. A pan of hot cooking oil, in his day, was for the face of a nonce, not for cooking fancy meals in prison cookery class.

'I'm just a pawn in a game. That's why they continue to shout my name.' Once upon a time, the name Kray would send the fear of God up the backs of the underworld. But time passed and, after Reg had been inside for some years, the Kray name became simply a curio. Anyone hearing the name 'Kray' shouted in prison would crane their necks just to get a look at one of them, just out of curiosity, as the fear factor had gone.

Every so often, the Prison Service would leak details of Reg's condition to the press. As I mention elsewhere, even Reg's wedding photos were released to the press without his knowledge; they were supposed to be in the safe care of the Prison Service.

'They'll make sure I do each day. Because I'm Reg Kray.' Yeah, sure! Reg knew he was a trophy to every new home secretary. But he had the last laugh when he was given 'compassionate parole' by Jack Straw. An article appeared in a newspaper saying that Reg had duped the Prison Service and that he was really fully fit. Jack Straw must have been shitting bricks at this story, which wasn't true, but it gave Reg a chuckle or two.

'No they will not like what I have to say. Because my name is Reg Kray.' Every time Reg gave money to charity, no one cared about running the story, but the minute they could demonise Reg Kray, they were there, shit hot! The Kray name was connected to infamy and bad deeds. Reg knew this, but he just couldn't get it working in his favour. No one wanted to hear how much of a nice man Reg was, and that's what cost him his parole chances early on. He knew this, but what could he do?

DAWN OF TOMORROW

The dawn of tomorrow holds no sorrow
There will be joy on each day
I just know it's going to be that way
Sunshine will come down from the sky
To begin each day
Today will be yesterday's memory
Tomorrow today's dream
Happiness will be our theme
That will be today for you and me
Each moment the full joy of a day
Because you make it this way
Each moment a dream
Our joy will be naturally
Because our path is free
There's no weeds in our way
That's the way it should be
Each moment a rose of happiness
Which makes every day bliss
And life a dream for you and me
Join me in my happiness and joy be my theme
You are part of my dream
Let it be this way
Just you and me
Let's live today and share this dream
Just you and me.

The last of the selected poems from *Thoughts* is poignant. I believe this poem shows what Reg was really like. OK, it's not a classic poem, but we are here at Reg's invitation to be analytical. So let's see what we can make of it.

'Today will be yesterday's memory. Tomorrow today's dream.' A great little saying – I don't know if Reg picked this up from somewhere or whether he invented it himself. What do these two lines mean and what did Reg mean by them? He's saying, forget whatever happened yesterday, we all make mistakes; just put your hope in tomorrow, as you never know what might come along to surprise you.

'Because our path is free. There's no weeds in our way'. That's the way it should be. Remember Reg's definition of a friend: 'It is said that a man is judged by the company he keeps, so in effect, it is better to have a bed of roses rather than a garden of weeds.' All enemies are swept away, his route is now clear of all obstacles, which was his downfall when his so-called friends became turncoats. In a perfect world there wouldn't be such obstacles, as that is the way it should be. Reg never forgave those in the Firm who turned lemon!

'You are part of my dream. Let it be this way. Just you and me. Let's live today and share this dream. Just you and me.' Reg had a way of making people feel special. His 'you and me' saying made it seem that there was no one else in the world he would rather have with him. I can see how Roberta fell for his charms and how he had a way with words when it came to business dealings. Reg could make it seem that whoever he was talking to, about whatever subject matter, was the only person in the world he wanted to tell it to – he really was that kind of man. He made his friends feel special. Pity some of them didn't return the kindness …

A great little book, *Thoughts*! So don't let no one ever tell you otherwise! Should you be able to get a copy and read the contents, then you will have found the key to what really made Reg tick.

Remember, that book was written before people jumped on the 'true crime' bandwagon and hyped things up. Hey, don't go thinking that I'm one of those doing the hyping! If anything, I play things down. I can back up everything I have said. My whole life within prison is logged. I have no need to tell tall tales.

Reg was a matter-of-fact guy. He had no need to hype anything up. He too played a lot of things down, although he didn't do himself any favours in some of his later books by admitting to doing and enjoying doing certain crimes. I put these 'author confessions' of Reg down to having done too much time and neglecting his own interests. He had a lot to lose by doing this; he lost 32 years and paid for it with his life. Who wants to be the next Reg Kray?

A final contribution from Joe Pyle, taken from his book *Looking at Life*, says it all.

We're jailed and classed as double 'A'
In the special unit we have to stay
It's a factory for problems one might agree
Where man's only aim is to be set free

A man must be strong and stand up to the screws
For the strong will survive and the weaker will lose
Now one doesn't fail just by hitting rock bottom
If he doesn't climb back though he's soon forgotten

It's said that a good lawyer has plenty of punch
But the clever one, though,
takes the judge out to lunch
Our freedom's not missed 'til it's taken away
The same as the air we breathe every day

For nobody knows what the future will tell
Why wait 'til you're thirsty to dig that well.

CHAPTER 11

DEATHBED CONFESSION

After spending nearly 33 years behind bars for the murder of Jack 'the Hat' McVitie, on compassionate grounds and with only days to live, Reggie was released from prison in August 2000.

Inoperable cancer of the bladder was to be the key to Reg's release, but was also to be the killing of him. Reg went through two operations to rid him of the cancerous growths that had spread from his bladder, but nothing could be done to save him.

Reg's lawyer, Trevor Linn, wrote to the Home Secretary, 'I have now been informed by Mr Kray's treating consultant that Mr Kray has cancer of the bladder with other secondary tumours. The consultant's opinion is that Mr Kray could have days rather than weeks to live. His condition is terminal. The cancer is inoperable and will not respond to chemotherapy.'

After Reg passed away, Roberta wrote in the final chapter to Reg's last book that, if the cancer had been found when Reg complained of stomach pains, he might have been saved by early treatment.

When you consider that the likes of the legendary underworld figure of Harry Marsden overcame the big 'C' (he underwent major surgery for cancer of the stomach) and how – now in his sixties – he runs his own boxing club, then that claim by Roberta could well be true.

In the USA, cancer of the bladder is the fourth most common malignancy among males and the tenth most common malignancy among females. Each year in the States, more than 12,000 people die of cancer of the bladder, which usually occurs in people over the age of sixty. (Reg was 67 when he died.) Reg loved a cigarette, and cigarette smoking, along with exposure to certain industrially used chemicals, is strongly associated with the development of bladder cancer.

The most common symptom of cancer of the bladder is blood in the urine (known as haematuria). This usually occurs suddenly and is generally not painful, although Reg was, at times, in immense pain – which leads me to believe that the cancer was quite advanced by that time. Blood in the urine may be present one day and disappear the next, but eventually it does come back. The cause of Reg's immense pain would have been attributed to blood clots, which would have been the cause of painful muscle spasms in the bladder. At this stage, Reg should have had a full medical. Instead, he was diagnosed as suffering from Irritable Bowel Syndrome! This more than anything is the reason I do not trust prison doctors or medical staff. I would rather be seen by a vet!

As Reg lay on his deathbed in the Norfolk and Norwich Hospital, he contributed to a one-hour BBC TV documentary, in which he admitted to committing another murder, though he never said where Frank Mitchell's body was disposed of.

Also interviewed on the BBC1 programme were Roberta, Reg's barrister John Platts Mills QC, and several of the Kray Firm.

During the filming, Reg was asked if he had committed any more murders, other than that of Jack 'the Hat' McVitie. He replied: 'One, one.' Although Reg wouldn't name the victim, retired Detective Chief Superintendent Leonard 'Nipper' Read shed some light on it when he said, 'I should imagine that would be Teddy Smith – he suddenly disappeared [in 1967].'

When asked, on his deathbed, about how he felt about his past crimes, Reg said: 'It is very difficult to apologise in some cases but not in others. But I suppose if I've been a bit too violent over the years I make some apologies about it, but there's little I can do about it now, so again, it's no good reflecting back. It's pointless, negative.'

On 23 September, Reg was determined to go out of the world in style. He was whisked away from hospital in a staged ploy – a cream-coloured Rolls-Royce was used to dupe the press into making them believe he was in it. While they were pursuing the Roller, Reg slipped quietly out of the hospital back door and spent his final days in the Honeymoon Suite of the three-star Beefeater Townhouse Hotel with Roberta.

Reg could see the river view from his hotel window, but his dream of walking in the hotel grounds with Roberta would never be possible. In the final days, Reg was kept under heavy sedation, and, along with the anti-sickness drugs, he drifted in and out of sleep.

On the final day, against the wishes of Roberta, some underworld associates from Reg's past visited him and were with him until he died in his sleep on 1 October 2000.

Some say Reg died in his sleep but, in reality, he died years earlier when Ron passed away. It wasn't long before the vultures were out to take stock of what they could pick at. A claim was soon made that Reg the once-feared underworld figure was gay and that he kept a string of secret young prison lovers. It was even claimed that if Reg took a liking to any new prisoners then he would pester them for sex. Although Reg did ask for an AIDS test (it came back negative), this is a common fear amongst prisoners; there are a million reasons why a prisoner might request an AIDS test.

It was also claimed that Reggie received an underworld tip-off while behind bars that three former lovers were threatening to expose his gay leanings. But it seems odd that it was also stated that Reg feared he would be branded 'a poof'. This seems to go along the same imaginary story that was made up about Ron allegedly reacting to being called 'a big fat poof', which was incorrectly claimed to have been the reason for him killing George Cornell. Someone tried to tie the twins into the same 'poof' fairy tale story.

Right to the very end, Reg was in the limelight ... even on his deathbed! What his 'Free Reg Kray' campaign team failed to do, Reg managed to do himself: he gained the world's attention with a deathbed confession. Reg was clever: he didn't name his alleged victim – he had nothing to lose at that stage by naming names, but he didn't, simply because he couldn't bring himself to name anyone. What it demonstrated was showmanship: Reg knew how to put on a show and he knew how to fill the seats.

With Reg's book *A Way of Life* coming out after his death, he had to have a selling point; he didn't want to leave Roberta with nothing. Although it was claimed by Reg's lawyer that he died penniless, I do not believe this to be the case! Reg was a shrewd businessman with a clever head on his shoulders. Plenty of Reg's money went to help people get on in life; he always had a return on this investment, even if it was just a favour or two in return.

CHAPTER 12

THE KRAY
CONNECTION

I want to reveal something very personal, something that you might, or might not, be able to understand: Reg Kray is responsible for what I have become! 'WHAT?' I hear you gasp. What I mean is that Reg Kray played the most important role in helping me to become a bare-knuckle fighter and that my fighting name came about as a direct result of Reggie's opening doors and helping find me a boxing manager.

Would I have remained just plain 'Michael Peterson' without Reggie's involvement in my life? Who knows? But I will say this: I wouldn't change one moment of it. Obviously I have held the memory of the Krays very close to me. There are certain admissions made to me by Reg and Ron that I have not revealed, as there are people still living who would suffer as a consequence.

I cannot reveal the names of those involved in

disposing of certain bodies, etc. I cannot reveal the names of those people employed by the Krays to carry out their orders while they were behind bars. But I can reveal that the Krays only targeted those that deserved such actions.

In response to a certain character revealing that Ron asked him to kill Kate Kray, all I will say is this: ha, ha, ha, ha, ha, ha, ha! Wake up and smell the coffee! Ron may have been pulling his leg – after all, if he wanted anyone dead then he had a whole list of professional hit men he could have drawn upon to have anyone he wanted put away. The funny thing is, how come it was only after the death of Reg and Ron that this man said he had felt the compunction to write a book about the Krays?

The Krays were dinosaurs, legends, icons and historical culture all rolled into one. The likes of the Krays will never be seen again in our lifetimes, you can be assured of that.

I recently heard one of the most stupid things I've ever heard: someone is claiming to be the third twin! This third Kray geezer is, supposedly, living out in Spain. Can you believe such idiocy? This goon says he made off while the going was good after the Krays made a fortune. If you believe this then you will also believe in the tooth fairy. Any Kray worth his salt would not have deserted his brothers; they were truly brothers in arms.

Take a look at the photos in this book and see how

the Krays influenced me. See the photos of Tony McCullough and me sparring in Hull Prison in 1999. Don't those photos tell you something? Don't they give you hope that someone like me can be rehabilitated under their own steam? 'Cos if I have to wait for the prison authorities to spend a little time on me then I might as well wait until the earth burns up on its way to the sun.

The Krays gave me hope. Hope that even after 32 years of imprisonment you can actually get out of prison to live your dream, even if for only a few weeks like Reg managed.

I don't ask any favours and, just like the Krays, I will not bow down to win freedom. I would rather die like a man than a dog begging for a bone. I don't want any handouts, just as the Krays didn't want any.

Before the Lottery Commission came along, the Krays were one of the main sources of handouts for people looking to make a new start. That's what influenced me to become a giver. I give to charities just as the Krays did; I give as much as I can. But I will have a long way to go to catch up to the hundreds of thousands of pounds given away to the many good causes by the twins.

* * * * *

It is now 2004; I have served thirty years, the same amount as the tariff set for the twins, so it's quite apt that this book should be written on my own thirtieth. anniversary!

I hope I have, at least, cleared up some bad stigmas and exposed some rats. And I also hope all you leeches die screaming in agony. Because you are not fit to clean the Krays' shoes. Me, I have never tried to make myself out to be anything. After all, to most people, I remain a lunatic.

If I had lived in the Capone era, I would still not have been in the Firm. Simply because I do what I do alone, my way. I show the chaps respect. I wish you all well! But, I actually believe you're all dragged down by managers and ripped up by media.

I do prefer to live my life on the edge, so, if and when I fall, I fall alone. Nobody is invincible. And all the big firms ended up with big-time porridge. Go ask Ronnie Biggs how he feels. Is it all worth it? Was it worth it with the twins and Charlie? Only they could answer that.

Many have put me down as a loser: 'How can Bronson fight, he's a nobody.' 'Bronson can't box.' 'What training has Bronson done, he'll get killed in the ring.' Well, let me tell you the training I've done! Just take a look at some of the photos in this book; you'll see some of me when I was sparring in Hull Prison. I've also got Harry Marsden on my team, he'll add the finishing touches to my boxing training when I'm free. Harry's a legend up North and my secret weapon!

We all got to do what we do, I guess, like when I climb

into the ring with Crazy Horse and all the faces are cheering me on, and my pals are behind me: Joe Pyle, Freddie Foreman, Roy Shaw, Ray Williams, Ed Clinton, Chris Reed, Andy Jones, Mark Rahim, Charlie and Eddie Richardson, Tel Currie, Frank Fraser, Harry Batt, Harry Marsden, Steve Richards, Maz Bradley, Alfie Lodge, Johnny Bristow, Tony Bowels, Craig Bulger, Jim Brookes, John Blake, Dave Courtney, Ron Critchley, Paddy Conroy, Bernie Davies, Micky Ahmed, Stevie Cooley, Jim Dawkins, Jason Dawes, Robert Eringer, Carl Dawson, Dave Ford, Mickey Holland, Eddie Holland, Kevin Houston, Wayne Rigby, Ray Light, Mark Lilliott, John Markey, Matthew Mark, Tony McCullough, Danny Marcovitch, Dougie Maynard, Redd Menties, Sharkie O'Connor, Dougie Maynard, Chris Power, Satpal Ram, Paddy Joe Hill, Darren Ramsey, Dominic Noonan, Reeds, Swellbellys, Tony Simpson, Paul Smith, Stilks, Paul Stevenson, John Wilson, Kevo Brown, Johnny Walker, Brian Fielding and Cass Pennant.

Fuck me, I can go on and on. Believe me, it will be a major event, they're coming for me, not Horsley. Who's Horsley? I rest my case!

A good friend of mine, Tel Currie, held a boxing charity night in my honour on 26 February 2004. Part of the money raised in a charity auction I contributed to went towards helping a young girl in need of treatment. But will the parole board or appeal courts give me credit? Will Tel get a knighthood? All of the old Kray associates were there supporting the event – some I will not mention, as they are not worthy of mention. Tel and Julian Davies have written a great book called *Bouncers*, all about club doormen around the country. Now that book would have amused Ron and Reg!

I intend to follow this boxing up when I'm released. I intend to follow the Kray tradition of having a boxing event tied in with all the trimmings and fund raising for the needy – watch me fight as you tuck into a medium-rare steak! My good pal Harry Marsden, the original Geordie Mafia and well-respected Newcastle under-world figure, will help all of this along.

So many people put me down, just as they put the Krays down. But do not underestimate my resolve. Rudolf Hess lived into his nineties before he died in Spandau Prison. I intend to be out to freedom long before I'm in my nineties.

Look at the condition I'm in – would you go six rounds with me for charity? Would you have gone six rounds with Ron or Reg? I bet not! Don't send in your CV, as I have already got my first fight lined up – Richy Horsley, I'm ready for you!

* * * * *

The cultural influence the Krays exerted in the Sixties is beyond the comprehension of most people. Unless you lived amidst their aura then you would not be able to fully appreciate what they were really like. I am able to empathise with this era due to spending a lot of time with all three of the Kray brothers. Some people, even to this day, try and emulate the Krays – flash suits and flash cars. But I have a little secret to tell you regarding all that: the Kray twins liked nothing better than lounging around and, at times, slumming it – yeah! Hope that hasn't blown the myth away too much! All of the people walking around with a Kray chip on their shoulder will now look a bit of prat, especially since shiny suits have long since been history. (Mind you, spandex is still in, so why not wear a spandex suit and look a double prat!)

The Kray methodology still exists to this day, but no one can really pull it off with such panache as the Krays did. You see, to pull off the Kray style you have to dispense with the hard man deep voice and the twenty-inch biceps. You don't need twenty-inch biceps to pull a trigger. What the Krays had was something that can't be taught. Young upstarts can model it, but they suffer from burnout. Ron could drink all night, right through to the following morning, and then carry on as normal without losing sight of what the day had in store for him. Nowadays, they can't even hold their own against the drugs they take to create an artificial luminance of amusement.

What really gets me is how all of the people who hold the Kray name on high have lost sight of what really made the Krays tick. We've got everything from the 'they only hurt those on the wrong side of the fence' brigade to those who say 'the Kray days were when you could leave your front door open with the key in it without anything being stolen'.

Well, let me tell you something: the days when people left their keys in their doors and their doors open were when they didn't have videos, CD players, stacking systems and fancy TV sets! They had bugger all to be stolen. Try asking the tobacconists or off-licences that were around in the Kray days if they dared to leave their doors open! Admittedly, the Kray name did deter sneak thieves and the likes of them, but that was it. You still had the likes of Freddie Foreman, a Kray associate, doing his ram raids on commercial outlets.

Mind you, you wouldn't have found a solitary paedophile living within their vicinity – they would have had a quiet word in their ear, and that is all it would have taken. The predominance of paedophilic activities and child murders has increased since the days of the Krays. As I've made plain in this book, that sort of crime was abhorrent to the Krays and their associates. The sad thing is, Ron had to tolerate a lot of this sort of filth when he was in Broadmoor, as I had to. Ron's ideology when in Broadmoor was so long as they didn't cross his line and as long as they cast their eyes down to the ground in his presence, then that was fine.

Issues such as having to learn how to operate computers were not even thought of in the days of the Krays. How things have changed. Something that the Krays always possessed, though, was a head for numbers and making money. No one could pull a fast one on the Kray brothers when it came to counting pound notes.

Claims have been made that the Krays made millions from selling their own branded memorabilia. BOLLOCKS! OK, a few people bought the 'Free the Krays' bits and bobs that were for sale on their official website run by Mick Gallagher. Mick did a loyal and fine job for them, but neither he nor the Krays ever made millions from memorabilia sales. Too many people have been quick to make these claims – the very same jealous people who want to hype it all up out of proportion. To show how much bollocks it is, how many people do you know with 'Free the Krays' memorabilia? Very few, I would guess.

Then again, so long as there is a plethora of memorabilia and books relating to the Krays knocking about then the Kray connection will always be around. Just to show you how long that connection could go on for, look back at the stories of the Roman generals. To this day, thousands of years on, these people are remembered, just as the Krays will be remembered in thousands of years' time. There are that many books out about the Krays, but this book is the final piece of the jigsaw, the one to fill in the missing gaps.

I set my sights to hold the same moral code as the Krays held: no hurting women, children, the infirm or the elderly. This set of unwritten rules was set deep in the minds of the Krays. Only women beaters and child molesters were branded by hot irons, others got a slapping and the real bad people were disposed of. The Krays were solely responsible for transforming the British gangland scene. Where they walked, others could only watch in awe!

* * * * *

Since the Kray gang have gone, many have tried to exert a similar influence across London, but all have failed. I don't want to mention the names of these failed crime families, as they do not deserve to be mentioned in the same breath as the Krays.

Even though the Krays have gone, they still continue to exert an influence over their followers. The legend of the Krays will continue to fascinate people, and now that you've learned something about the Krays and me, I hope my first-hand observations have helped maintain the Krays' place in criminal folklore.

For all of those who witnessed the dying Reg Kray shrunken to a shadow of his former self, do not believe that this was the man as he had been in the Sixties. And even though Reg's body was riddled with cancer, he still had the inner strength not to be remorseful over anything he did.

The government of the day were rocked by the extent of the Krays' power, and that is why certain public records are not available to the general public. I mean, look at the Public Records Office's list of documents relating to the Krays and see how much is missing. Why have these files been pulled?

Did you know that the Krays were to be prosecuted over stolen bonds, but that the case never proceeded due to the Krays being convicted over the Cornell/McVitie murders? Even a royal connection to the twins saw the slapping of a banning order stopping the public having access to the 'Royal Dossier'. That is the extent of how far the Kray tentacles of power reached, and still reach to this day.

Since the death of the Kray brothers, plenty of people have spread false propaganda about them. Anyone can claim this and that about the dead 'cos they aren't here to defend themselves once they've passed away. So think about that! Why speak ill of the dead? Wait 'til you meet them face to face!

Me, I'm just a small part of a very big story, an as-yet incomplete story … but we'll have to wait fifty years for the real truth to come out, as that's when the gagging order is lifted from the banned Kray files.

No doubt, by then, some bright spark will be working on the Broadway musical about the Krays. Save me a ticket, I'll see you there!

KRAY FACT FILE

BIRTH, GROWING UP AND DEATH

First birth: In 1927, Violet Kray gave birth to Charles David (after she had been expecting twins), at the first family home in Gorusch Street in Hackney. Charlie's first job was as a messenger for Lloyds of London!

Second birth: Expecting to give birth to one child, Violet gave girth to two babies... Reggie and Ronnie.

First born: Reggie, at 8am, on Tuesday, 24 October 1933. He was followed ten minutes later by Ronnie.

Twins' birth sign: Scorpio.

Place of twins' birth: 68 Stean Street, London's East End (near Hoxton, now known as Shoreditch).

Schooling: By the age of twelve, the twins were attending Daniel Street School – Reggie excelled in English and Ronnie took to general knowledge like a duck to water.

Violet dies: The mother of the Kray twins died of cancer in 1982.

Violet's funeral: Violet Kray is buried on 11 August 1982. Both Ronnie and Reggie attend, with a high-security presence under secure escort.

Ronnie marries: In 1985, the homosexual Ron surprised everyone when he married Elaine Mildener. Elaine had actually started up her acquaintanceship with the twins by writing to and visiting Ron's brother Reggie.

Ronnie divorces: The marriage to Elaine was doomed to failure, and in 1989 they were divorced.

Ronnie remarries: To the surprise of all, in 1990, Ronnie married divorcée and ex-Kissogram girl Kate Howard in Broadmoor. Originally, Kate met Reg on a visit to Gartree when she was visiting someone else; he asked her to take some letters to Ron. Romance blossomed and Ron asked her to marry him on only her second visit.

Ronnie Divorces: In 1994, Ronnie and Kate divorced, although Kate kept her marital name of 'Kray'.

Ronnie dies: On 17 March 1995, Ronnie Kray died from a massive heart attack in hospital two days after he collapsed in his ward at Broadmoor Special Hospital at 09.07 GMT after being transferred to Wexham Park Hospital, Slough, from Heatherwood Hospital in Ascot. Reggie had suffered two earlier heart attacks; doctors warned him that his 100-cigarettes-a-day habit would eventually kill him.

Reggie remarries: On the afternoon of 14 July 1997,

Reg married wife number two, Roberta Jones, in the chapel of Maidstone Prison.

Charlie dies: On 4 April 2000, Charlie Kray died in hospital as an inmate. Crowds flocked to his funeral service on 19 April 2000.

Reggie Kray dies: On 1 October 2000, Reggie Kray, a free man, died of cancer. He had been granted compassionate parole after being diagnosed as terminally ill, having served 32 years of a thirty-year recommended prison sentence. On 11 October, Reggie was buried in Chingford Mount Cemetery in the same grave as his twin brother, Ron.

Family burial plot: Chingford Mount Cemetery, Essex, London.

Frances Kray's Suicide: On 7 June 1967, Frances's brother found her dead in bed; this was her third suicide attempt. An inquest at the time concluded Frances Kray had committed suicide by taking an overdose of phenobarbitone.

Reggie fell into a deep depression, blaming Frances's parents for his wife's death. He felt so strongly about this that he wanted to kill them, but knew he could not do something that Frances could not have countenanced. What followed was a shooting spree in which Reggie shot and wounded a man he believed had insulted his wife. In another incident, Reggie shot a man named Freddie Fields in the leg at a club at Highbury after demands and threats failed to get money from him.

In 2002, Bradley Allardyce, formerly Reggie Kray's

gay prison lover, claimed that Reggie had spilled his heart out to him in prison. Allardyce alleged that one of these revelations by Reggie was that twin brother Ronnie murdered Frances.

FAMILY

Heritage: Hungarian and Romany as well as Irish and Gypsy blood from the 'Lee' family side; the Jewish side of the family stemmed from paternal grandfather 'Mad Jimmy''s heritage.

Great-grandfather (maternal): 'Creecha' Lee spent the last two decades of his life in an asylum. His insanity was thought to have been brought about by his alcoholism.

Grandfather (paternal): 'Mad Jimmy', a stallholder on London's Brick Lane.

Grandfather (maternal): 'Johnny the Southpaw Cannonball' Lee, a bare-knuckle fighter and light heavyweight boxer. Eventually travelled as a music-hall balancing act, then went on to become a market porter.

Mother: Violet Annie (maiden name: Lee) came from Bethnal Green, London. Ran away from home at the age of seventeen (1926) to marry Charlie Kray, in London's Kingsland Road Register Office.

Father: Charlie was what was called a 'totter' (rag and bone man).

Second address: 178 Valance Road (nicknamed 'Fort Valance'), Bethnal Green, London. Family moved here in 1939.

Reggie weds: On 20 April 1965, at St James' Church, in Bethnal Green, Reggie and Frances Shea were married. On their return from honeymooning in Athens, Reggie and Frances rented an expensive apartment directly below Ronnie's place, just off Lancaster Gate in the West End.

Eventually, after eight weeks, Reggie was spending more time with Ronnie than he was with Frances and being made a prisoner in her own home gave Frances the impetus to return home to live with her parents.

After suffering the symptoms of a nervous break-down and with her marriage in tatters, Frances visited a top Harley Street specialist – the same one used by Ronnie Kray!

Reggie was never allowed in to visit his wife at his in-laws' home, so he would stand outside on the pavement and talk to Frances as she leaned out of the second-storey bedroom window. Frances sometimes mentioned getting an annulment of the marriage, but she never pursued it.

In October 1966, Frances attempted to take her own life by gassing herself – just in time, her father found her and she survived. Reggie and Frances then went on a second honeymoon to Ibiza, but the writing was by this time already on the wall.

ILLNESS

First serious illness: At the age of three, both twins suffered from diphtheria, further compounded by a bout of the measles. Ronnie also had a hernia.

First hospitalisation: Both twins, as a consequence of the diphtheria, were admitted to hospital; Reggie to St Anne's at Tottenham and Ronnie to Homerton.

First disparity from being identical twins: After the hospitalisation, it became apparent that Ronnie was a little slower than Reggie and was now heavier set.

First diagnosis of mental illness: Ronnie was diagnosed as suffering from Prison Psychosis while at Winchester Prison.

Classified as insane: On 28 December 1957, Ronnie was officially classified as insane.

First time admitted to a lunatic asylum: On 20 February 1958, Ronnie was removed from Winchester Prison and driven by ambulance to Long Grove Hospital, Surrey, London, where he was diagnosed as having suffered a schizophrenic breakdown.

TEENAGE LAWLESSNESS

First taste of law and order: The twins' father was conscripted to the Army in 1939, and for twelve years, until 1952, he was a deserter. The first encounter with police coming to arrest their father set the mould: henceforth the twins perceived the police as the 'baddies'.

Reggie's first run-in with the law: On a train travelling home from Chingford at the age of twelve, Reggie fired an air gun out of the window. The magistrates' court let him off with a warning. Feeling badly done by, Reggie took offence at the court appearance; he was now well and truly at odds with the law.

Ronnie's first run-in with the law: Along with brother Reggie, Ronnie was arrested at the age of sixteen for an attack on three youths: Roy Harvey, Dennis Seigenberg (who later changed his name to Dennis Stafford and was to be convicted of the infamous 'body in the boot' murder, a brutal gangland killing that inspired the classic British crime thriller *Get Carter*) and Walter Birch. After being charged with grievous bodily harm, Reggie and Ronnie were sent on to the High Court by North London Magistrates' Court. Due to lack of evidence, the case was dismissed.

Ronnie and Reggie's second run-in with the law: One week after their first pro boxing bouts, the twins were arrested for assaulting a policeman. Ronnie was arrested after causing a mêlée outside a café with some other youths. The arrest came after he was poked in the stomach by the policeman and told to move on. Ronnie snapped and instantly threw a punch to the policeman's jaw. After Ronnie ran off, the policeman gave chase, caught him and marched him quietly to Bethnal Green police station. Ronnie was charged and released, but on hearing of how Ronnie was beaten up on the police station, Reggie went out in search of the policeman. When he eventually found the policemen, Reggie was given a graphic account of how Ronnie was beaten up. On hearing these boasts, Reggie did the same to the policeman as Ronnie (threw a punch to his jaw), and he too ran off.'

After a lengthy stand-off, Reggie was arrested. The

twins received probation and were fortunate to be able to hang on to their pro boxing licences.

Reggie escapes from Long Grove Hospital (lunatic asylum): In late May 1958, whilst Ronnie was serving a three-year prison sentence (see 'Prison' section later), Reggie and a friend, George Osborne, visited Ronnie. The twins switched places and Ronnie escaped.

PRISON AND THE POLICE

Ronnie's first time in a straightjacket: Christmas Day, 1957. Ronnie's Aunt Rose (one of the twins' favourites) died and two days later, while banged up in Winchester Prison, Ronnie learned of the news and went berserk. He had to be placed in a straightjacket for his own safety.

Tower of London used to cage up the Krays: On 2 March 1952, the twins were called up for their two-year mandatory National Service. They reported to Waterloo Barracks at the Tower of London and were assigned to the Royal Fusiliers.

They absconded back home, knocking out a corporal on the way, but were arrested within 24 hours and returned to the Tower, where they were held to face a punishment of seven days in the guardroom.

Further leaves without permission resulted in Ronnie being held back at the Tower (in Wellington Barracks) while Reggie was sent to Purfleet, where he served time in the Fusiliers' punishment cells. In an attempt to convince his commanding officers that he was mad, and get himself ousted from the Army, Ronnie shaved half his face and indulged in several other bizarre acts.

Colchester Military Detention Barracks: The twins spent a month here and then, again, absconded. This routine of absconding and being arrested was an ongoing thing, until, during a spell on the run, they pushed a policeman over a wall.

HMP Wormwood Scrubs: January 1953 saw the Kray twins spend a month here due to the aforementioned assault on a policeman who had been trying to take them in for absconding from the Army.

Howe Barracks Guardroom, Canterbury: After serving their one-month civil prison sentence, the twins were put under 'close arrest' for three months to await trial for absconding. During their incarceration they made an escape bid, although they were caught soon after breaking out.

Shepton Mallet Military Prison: Sentenced to nine months for their misbehaviour in the Army, the twins were dishonourably discharged from the army in 1954.

Ronnie shoots his first man: In the autumn of 1956, a car dealer asked Ronnie for protection from an irate customer demanding his money back for a duff car. After a brief struggle, the customer was shot in the leg with Ronnie's Luger pistol.

Although the victim identified Ronnie as the attacker, the accused man swore he was not Ronnie but Reggie! Embarrassed police at Arbour Square police station released him and withdrew the charges.

HM Prison Wandsworth, London: On Friday, 5 November 1956, Ronnie started a three-year sentence for a tit-for-tat assault on Terence Martin. Although Reggie was charged along with Ronnie, he was acquitted.

HM Prison Camp Hill, Isle of Wight: Six months on from receiving his three-year sentence, Ronnie was transferred well away from London.

HMP Winchester: Concerned at his mental state, the prison authorities transferred Ronnie to the psychiatric wing of HMP Winchester, where he was diagnosed as having 'prison psychosis'.

Long Grove Hospital, Surrey: In February 1958, Ronnie was transferred from prison and diagnosed as suffering from a schizophrenic breakdown. After his escape in June, Ronnie became even more uncontrollable and attempted suicide. The rest of the Krays made a decision against all that they believed in: they contacted Scotland Yard and the next morning, at 2am, they collected Ronnie.

HM Prison Wandsworth: After a brief spell at Long Grove, Ronnie was deemed fit enough to complete his sentence. He returned to prison and was discharged in the spring of 1959. This was not the same man who had started his sentence – he was moodier and had lost the Reggie look. By now, Ronnie had changed physically and was no longer an identical twin.

HM Prison Wandsworth: In 1960, it was Reggie's turn to visit prison – for eighteen months. Reggie had demanded money with menaces when he used the ploy of demanding a refund of £100 for a leather briefcase in what he claimed was overcharging by the shop. Of course, this was a scam used to extract money with menaces, but the police were waiting nearby and stepped in after Reggie head-butted the shopkeeper.

Housebreaking: A short time after being released from prison, Reggie was arrested on a charge of housebreaking. Not surprisingly, the woman who had originally made the complaint failed to identify Reggie in court. The case was dismissed.

Loitering with intent: On 8 May 1961, the twins appeared at Marylebone Magistrates' Court facing a charge of loitering with intent – a ludicrous charge brought about, said Ronnie, by a police vendetta against them. Eight witnesses were called, who provided the twins with a cast-iron alibi, and the case was dismissed. Ronnie felt he was cast-iron untouchable.

Demanding money with menaces: On 10 January 1965, the twins were arrested and charged with demanding money with menaces from Hew McCowan, the owner of a club in the West End called the Hideaway. The twins were remanded to prison awaiting trial. The trial started on 28 February, but the jury failed to reach an agreement, and a re-trial was ordered. Evidence was presented at the new trial that cast doubts against McCowan's character. The judge stopped the trial, finding for the defendants.

After the case was won, the twins held their biggest party ever – in McCowan's club! The twins had bought it and promptly renamed it the El Morocco. Even the police were invited along. The Krays really did seem untouchable.

Witness on the run: In June 1967, Ronnie was absent from Frances Kray's funeral; he was on the run, this time as a witness in an extortion charge involving the police.

Murder arrest: On 8 May 1968, the twins were arrested at their mother's flat, at Braithwaite House, Finsbury, and were among eighteen men held at West End Central police station, all helping with enquiries relating to offences of conspiracy to murder, fraud, demanding money with menaces and assault.

McVitie verdict: On 4 March 1969, the twins were found guilty of murdering Jack 'the Hat' McVitie.

Life sentences all round: In March 1969, life sentences were passed on the twins with a recommendation that they serve at least thirty years. Ron was shipped to Durham Jail and Reg to Parkhurst Jail.

Charlie is Charlie's downfall: In June 1997, after a police undercover operation, Charlie was found guilty of masterminding a £39 million cocaine supply chain; he received a death sentence jail term of twelve years.

BOXING CAREERS

First boxing gym attended by the twins: Robert Browning Youth Club's Gym, South London, where they were coached by Charlie Simms.

School days end: At the age of fifteen, both twins leave school and go to work at Billingsgate Fish Market,

London – Reggie as a trainee salesman, and Ronnie as an 'empty boy', searching the market each day and collecting the empty discarded fish boxes.

Charlie's dreams: His hopes of winning the Lonsdale Belt as boxing champion of the world never came to fruition.

Reggie's schoolboy record: In 1948, Reggie was the Schoolboy Boxing Champion of Hackney. The top accolade of becoming the London Schoolboy Champion went to Reggie in the same year. The best achievement of the young Reggie was reaching, but not winning, the finals in the Great Britain Schoolboys event.

Ronnie's record: Although not as illustrious as his older twin, in comparison, he brawled his way to winning similar accolades as Reggie and went on to win the Keymer Cup for winning a Hackney boxing championship.

Fighting Ronnie: Although the two had fought each other in a fairground-boxing booth (a draw), Ronnie had beaten Reggie in 1946 and 1947 in the earlier rounds of the London Schoolboy Championships.

Three Kray brothers appear on the same boxing promotion: In December 1951, the Albert Hall, London, was the setting for the three brothers to appear on the same bill. Out of the three brothers, only Reggie was to win his bout.

Prison does not debar the twins from boxing: Although the spell behind bars in January 1953, as well as the nine months in Shepton Mallet Military Prison,

REGGIE'S PRO CAREER AS A LIGHTWEIGHT

The following record is taken from the website www.johnnyowen.com. It is not the definitive guide to all of Reggie's fights.

Won 7 (KOs 2)	Lost 0	Drawn 0	Tot 7		
Date	**Opponent**	**WLD**	**Location**		**Result**
11/12/1951	Bobby Manito	0-2-0	Kensington, London England		W PTS 6
19/11/1951	Bobby Woods	0-2-0	London, England		W PTS 6
29/10/1951	Bill Sliney	0-1-0	London, England		W PTS 6
22/10/1951	Bill Sliney	0-0-0-	London, England		W PTS 4
11/09/1951	George Goodsell	0-1-0	Wembley, London, England		W TKO 3
21/08/1951	Johnny Starr	0-1-0	London, England		W TKO 3
31-07-1951	Bobby Manito	0-1-0	London, England		W PTS 6

RONNIE'S PRO CAREER AS A LIGHTWEIGHT

The following record is taken from the website www.johnnyowen.com. It is not the definitive guide to all of Ronnie's fights.

Won 4 (KOs 4)	Lost 2	Drawn 0	Tot 6		
Date	**Opponent**	**WLD**	**Location**		**Result**
11/12/1951	Bill Sliney	0-2-0	Kensington, London, England		L PTS 6
19/11/1951	Doug Sherlock	0-2-0	London, England		L DQ 2
29/10/1951	George Goodsell	0-2-0	London, England		W KO 4
22/10/1951	Bobbie Edwards	0-1-0	London, England		W TKO 1
11/09/1951	Bernie Long	0-1-0	Wembley, London, England		W TKO 0
31/07/1951	Bernie Long	0-0-0	London, England		W TKO

CHARLIE'S PRO CAREER AS A WELTERWEIGHT

The following record is taken from the website www.johnnyowen.com. It is not the definitive guide to all of Charlie's fights.

Charlie carried out his National Service in the Royal Navy, where he continued his boxing as a welterweight.

After he was demobbed (discharged, medically unfit, because of severe migraine attacks) from the Royal Navy after World War II, he began a very fruitful pro boxing career, although he lacked the killer instinct of a champion.

Won 11 (KOs 0) | Lost 4 | Drawn 1 | Tot 16

Date	Opponent	WLD	Location	Result
11/12/1951	Lew Lazar	9-0-1	Kensington, London, England	L KO 3
29/09/1949	Len Brooks	5-3-0	Paignton, England	L PTS 6
05/05/1949	Ray Howard	0-0-0	Bournemouth, England	W PTS 6
23/04/1949	Dave Harris	0-0-0	Plymouth, England	L PTS 6
11/04/1949	Doug Eland	0-0-0	Walworth, London, England	W PTS 4
28/03/1949	Ron Delaney	0-0-0	Slough, England	W PTS 4
21/03/1949	Len Jones	0-6-0	Walworth, London, England	W PTS 4
14/03/1949	Tommy Slade	0-0-0	Kentish Town, London	L KO 1
08/03/1949	Leslie Wood	0 0 0	Watford, England	W PTS 3
08/03/1949	George Smith	0-0-0	Watford, England	W PTS 3
08/03/1949	Johnny Fraser	0-0-0	Watford, England	W PTS 3
27/01/1949	Vic Price	11-1-0	Poplar, England	W PTS 4
25/01/1949	Jimmy Blackburn	0-0-0	Epsom, England	D PTS 4
03/01/1948	Len Jones	0-5-0	Watford, England	W PTS 4
22/11/1948	Jack Allen	0-0-0	London, England	W PTS 4

CELEBRITIES, FRIENDS, ASSOCIATES
AND VISITORS TO THE CLUB

Atwell, Winifred: Piano player famous in the 1950s. Remained a great friend.

Bailey, David: Society and fashion photographer snapped the twins from the late 1950s and even attended Reg's wedding to Frances.

Bon Jovi, Jon: USA rock singer. Wrote to Ron.

Boothby, Lord: Inferred by newspapers as having a homosexual affair with Ronnie. Later, Lord Boothby accepted £40,000 from IPC, the Daily Mirror's parent company in compensation.

Bruno, Frank: UK-born former world champion boxer. Frequent visitor to the patients of Broadmoor.

Clapton, Eric: UK guitarist and singer. Made an early appearance at the beginning of his career at one of the Kray clubs, Esmeralda's Barn.

Collins, Jackie: Writer who used to frequent the Krays' Double R club.

Cooper, Henry: Former boxing champion. Opened one of the twins' boxing clubs.

Daltrey, Roger: Former Who band member. Became a supporter of Reggie.

Daniels, Billy: USA entertainer. Congratulated the twins on their taking over of The Cambridge Rooms

Dors, Diana: Iconic UK actress. A long-time supporter and friend of the Krays.

Effingham, Lord: Stood as a front man in the Krays' first club venture in the West End of London.

Essex, David: UK singer. Given his first singing break in the Kray club El Morocco.

Garland, Judy: USA actress and singer. Used to visit Ronnie but was also a frequent visitor to the Kray clubs.

Harry, Debbie: USA singer from the group Blondie. Visited Ron in Broadmoor.

Heston, Charlton: USA actor. Attended the Kray trial and wrote to Ron.

Keating, Helen: British actress. Remained friends with the Krays after growing up with them.

Kemp, Gary and Martin: UK singers, ex of Spandau Ballet, and actors. Played the role of the Kray twins in the film about them and visited Ron and Reg.

Kensit, Patsy: UK actress and singer. Reggie Kray was her godfather.

La Rue, Danny: Drag act star. Used to frequent the Krays' Double R club.

Lake, Alan: Actor, the husband of Diana Dors, who befriended the Krays.

Liston, Sonny: Boxer. Frequently in the company of the Krays during the Sixties.

Louis, Joe: Boxer. Frequently in the company of the Krays during the Sixties.

Lynch, Kenny: Entertainer. Grew up with the Krays, but never used this friendship to further his career.

Marciano, Rocky: World champion boxer. Kept in touch with the twins through their sentence.

Mortimer, Tony: Former boy band member of East 17. One of the pallbearers at Reggie's funeral.

Murray, Bill: UK soap star was a friend of the Krays.

Peters & Lee (Peters, Lennie and Lee, Di): Singing male and female duo who were helped along in their career because of the Krays – they were given their first break in one of the Kray clubs.

Pyle, Joe: Recording artists' manager, film production company owner and entrepreneur. Befriended the Krays in the early days and remained a loyal friend.

Raft, George: USA actor. Had business dealings with the twins and became a great friend.

Ray, Johnny: USA singer. Met the Krays in the Dolce Vita nightclub in Newcastle. Borrowed £10,000 from the Krays and stuck to his word of paying it back within four weeks.

Sheridan-Price, Eileen: A friend of the Krays since she met them when she won her 1958 Miss UK Crown

Sinatra, Frank Jr: The son of the famous crooner. Used to visit Ronnie.

Spinetti, Victor: UK actor. A frequent visitor to Ron in Broadmoor.

Tucker, Sophie: USA actress and singer.

Walker Brothers: Singers, made an appearance at the Kray club, Esmeralda's Barn.

White, Jimmy: UK snooker player. Regularly visited Ron at Broadmoor.

Windsor, Barbara: UK actress and star of *Carry On* series. Maintained her friendship with the Kray twins until they died.

Wisdom, Norman: UK actor. Wrote some of the funniest letters that Ron received at Broadmoor.

FEARS AND FAVOURITES

Reggie: Right back when Reggie was serving time for demanding money with menaces, he wrote an essay on the subject of why the death penalty should be abolished.

Ronnie: Feared the dark and being alone at night; as a child he shunned company in favour of spending time in the company of his Alsatian dog, Freda. In later life Ronnie became obsessively cautious. He would sleep with a gun under his pillow at night and leave the light on.

Reggie: Favourite song was Frank Sinatra's 'My Way', which was played at his funeral.

Ronnie: Favourite song (well, one of them) was 'My Yiddisher Mamma' by the Jewish-American singer Sophie Tucker.

QUIRKY FACTS

Actor in the making: Ron starred as a film extra in the big-screen movie *The Magic Box*.

Beginning of the end: The murder of Jack (real first name, John) 'the Hat' McVitie brought about a change of heart for a man called Leslie Payne. The twins had used violence against Payne and subsequently ruined him. A £250 bounty had been put on Payne's head, and Jack the Hat was the man Ronnie Kray had paid to carry out the hit. The failure to go ahead with the hit was to mark the beginning of the end for McVitie. Reggie stabbed him to death at a house party that had been organised purely for the purpose of killing McVitie.

After McVitie's death, the abortive plot to kill Payne spurred him on to realise that he needed to act and protect himself further against what lay around the corner … Ronnie and Reggie! By now, Payne was prepared to talk to Nipper Read. Secreted away during a three-week period, he sat and talked to Nipper, saying enough to fill over 200 pages with details of what he knew about the twins. This was the beginning of the end for the Kray twins.

Black Museum houses murder gun as trophy: The 9mm Mauser semi-automatic pistol used by Ronnie to kill Cornell was thrown into the River Lea; after it was recovered it was displayed in Scotland Yard's Black Museum.

Blind Beggar becomes *Blind Beggar*: The infamous killing ground of the Blind Beggar pub gained its name from an East End poem made into a play called The Blind Beggar of Bethnal Green.

Born to hang: Aunty Rose, the twins' favourite, commented to Ronnie, after he was teased at school about his eyebrows being too close together, that it was an omen that he was 'born to be hanged'. When Ronnie eventually came to trial for murder, he surely would have hanged had it not been for the relatively recent abolishment of capital punishment.

Box away the blues: After being sentenced to life, both Kray twins shadowboxed while held in the court holding cell.

Brain drain: The funeral service of Ronnie was to be his

THE KRAYS AND ME

first of two! The Home Office pathologist had removed his brain and secretly sent it for analysis. A second funeral had to be organised some months later to bury Ronnie's brain! Reggie was trying to organise an official inquiry into his brother's death before his own demise.

Castration (ouch): Ronnie toyed with the idea of using castration as a suitable form of punishment on some of the twins' enemies, but fortunately never found the opportunity to put his perverse conception into practice.

Christmas Day wedding: On Christmas Day, 1948, Charlie married his childhood sweetheart, Dorothy (Dolly) Moore.

Cornell the killer: Allegedly, George Cornell, murdered by Ron, admitted to the latter that he had killed a car dealer called Thomas 'Ginger' Marks in January 1965 in a drive-by shooting. Ron later said, 'I was only killing a killer.'

Crazy capers: Born 'Monek Prager' (alias Mickey Duff, boxing promoter) on 7 June 1929, with a strict Jewish upbringing. Many of his family were murdered at the Nazi death camps in Poland. Ronnie Kray (who was also of Jewish origin) had a twisted loathing of Mickey Duff and once referred to him as '... that bastard Mickey Duff, he's a slag and I once sent him a dead rat through the post; he deserved it. I should have killed him when I had the chance.'

Dinner with the Governor: While Frank Mitchell was serving time in Dartmoor Prison, Reg Kray disguised himself, used a moody name and, along with the boxer Ted 'Kid' Lewis, he visited Frank. The visit was an official one; boxing films were shown and Ted answered boxing questions. After the event, Ted and Reg had dinner with the grateful Governor, who told them not to forget to come back again!

Doh!: During a meeting with a top Mafia man, Angelo Bruno, at the London Hilton Hotel, the twins made an arrangement with the Philadelphia crime family.

About a year later, the Krays met a New York Mafia capo (crew boss) from the Lucchese family, Anthony 'Tony Ducks' Corallo. During one of the meetings with Tony Ducks, a small gift from the USA crime family was offered to the Krays. The gift was turned down. Had the Krays known about the $50,000 in the suitcase they were being offered, then perhaps this 'small' gift would not have been turned down!

Drink: In one night, it is claimed; Ronnie drank 55 bottles of beer without any trace of a hangover the next day.

Fight the good fight: The Kray madness seemed to have rubbed off from their Aunt Rose who had a fiery temper. She often would fight out in the street with other women.

Fun lovin' musical: In 1999, Reggie was teaming up with the bad-boy rap act Fun Lovin' Criminals for a new musical project.

Gypsy curse: At the request of Ron, a curse was put on Judge Melford Stevenson by gypsy Dot Welsh ... the judge went blind!

Hot poker fun: Granddad 'Southpaw Cannonball' Lee had a rather grisly party trick: stroking a white-hot poker over his tongue! Was this where the Kray twins learned their lessons of torture from? In one incident, Ron used a hot poker to brand a man who had beaten a woman; the man was scarred for life by Ron's hot poker fun. On another occasion, the woman beater broke a woman's nose in three places because she refused him sex.

Influential women: The twins' upbringing was notable for the absence of any strong masculine presence: their mother Violet, her two sisters and their grandmother brought them up.

Kray associate murder confession: Freddie Foreman, author of the best-selling book *Respect*, was once one of Britain's most notorious criminals, partly through his being a former associate of the Krays.

Somehow, a TV documentary managed to elicit a confession from Freddie that he'd been involved in murder and he admitted in the documentary that he had carried out at least two murders on the orders of the Krays. Detectives immediately launched a new investigation after he made his confession to millions of TV viewers. Under the 'double jeopardy' rule, he cannot be tried again for the murders.

Freddie confessed that a few months after he'd been involved in intimidating witnesses who had seen Ronnie Kray shoot George Cornell dead in Whitechapel's Blind Beggar pub in 1966, he took part in the killing of 'Mad

Axeman' Frank Mitchell. The CPS took no action over the TV confession.

During the Krays' Old Bailey trial in 1969, another gangland figure, Albert Donoghue, gave evidence against Freddie Foreman, the Kray twins and their brother Charlie. But the judge ruled that, because Donoghue was also involved in Mitchell's escape from prison, his evidence could not be accepted without corroboration. Freddie and the Krays were acquitted.

In a later admission, Ron Kray said some Greek men murdered Frank.

Marriages not consummated: Some say that Reg's marriage to his first wife, Frances, was never consummated, which begs the question as to how the other Kray marriages behind bars could have ever been consummated?

Nipper in the making: By the age of 36, Leonard 'Nipper' Read had become one of the youngest policemen to carry the rank of detective superintendent. As one of the top twelve detectives in the country, he was allowed to wear a very special tie, a globe pierced with a stiletto on a maroon background. This man would be the catalyst for the downfall of 'the Firm'. Having enjoyed such a rapid rise through the ranks, Nipper Read was almost a perfect choice as the man to bring the Krays to trial.

The 'hunt the Krays' season had now begun. Nipper Read brought in John du Rose, head of the Murder Squad, Superintendent Harry Mooney, Superintendent

Don Adams and Chief-Inspector Frank Cater – the latter became his personal assistant. Supported by fifteen other staff, they moved into offices at Tintagel House.

The Kray brothers had aspired to become boxing champs and, ironically, so had Nipper Read. He had come by his nickname 'Nipper' as a lightweight police boxing champion – the same weight that Reggie and Ronnie had fought at.

By the time Nipper Read appeared on the scene, the Krays had been active for twelve years: extorting, demanding, wounding, killing and committing other acts of a major criminal nature. The job of finding the weakest link lay with Nipper.

The Supergrass was about to be born; Nipper and du Rose had a long chat at Scotland Yard with top police lawyers and eventually persuaded them to accept the need to use criminals as a weapon.

Prison wedding photos: In a turnaround, the Home Office allowed Roberta Kray to use pictures of her husband in her 2002 biography *A Man Apart*. In contrast, a High Court action in 2004 by the wife of Charles Bronson to win the same concession with respect to her use of wedding photos of herself and her husband in her planned book was turned down!

Pulling for England: While held at Howe Barracks Guardroom, Canterbury, awaiting trial for absconding, it is claimed that Ronnie masturbated over a guard he had in his power.

Royal connection: Since the death of HRH Princess

CHARLES BRONSON

Margaret, it might be possible for certain information held on file linking her to visits she regularly made in the Sixties to a Kray gambling club to be released. In November 2000, nine police files were ordered to be kept under lock and key, and kept at the Public Records Office. Eight will remain locked away for fifty years and the ninth for thirty years.

The Government ordered the files to be locked away after a constituent expressed an interest in looking at them. The MP for Leyton and Wanstead, Harry Cohen, said: 'These files should be made public. This dossier is historic and should not be kept hidden.'

Singing away the blues: Although Violet had a great singing voice; she never used this to her advantage.

Smoke up: The twins acquired the lease to a billiard hall called The Regal, which had been converted from an old theatre and stood in Eric Street, off the Mile End Road in Bethnal Green. A special seat was put in place for Ron to sit and watch people coming in. He would hand out cigarettes to visitors and say, 'Smoke up. There's not enough smoke in here.'

Sucker punch: A favourite ploy by Reggie was to offer a man a cigarette with his right hand, and as the man concentrated on putting it into his mouth, Reggie would strike at the victim's jaw with a vicious left hook. Many of the victims' mouths were open ready to accept the cigarette, and an open jaw fractures easily!

The Sun Ain't Gonna Shine Anymore: On 8 March 1968, George Cornell was in the infamous Blind Beggar pub when Ronnie, accompanied by Ian Barrie, entered thc saloon bar. The jukebox was playing the Walker Brothers' 'The Sun Ain't Gonna Shine Anymore' when Cornell said, 'Well, look who's here now.' Ronnie pulled out a 9mm Mauser semi-automatic pistol, and shot Cornell in the head three times from point-blank range.

The jukebox was struck by a ricocheting bullet, causing the record to keep playing the same line of the song: 'The sun ain't gonna shine anymore ...'

You can leave your hat on: Jack 'the Hat' McVitie used a mixture of alcohol and pep pills called 'black bombers' to fuel his temper and give him a boost. He wore his hat to hide a bald spot – even when he was in the bath!

Vision: Both twins were short sighted.

KRAY QUOTES

REG KRAY

(on Ronnie): 'What can I do about Ron? He's ruining us. I know we should drop him. But how can I? He's my brother and he's mad.' (Reg was concerned about what Ronnie's behaviour was doing to their businesses after he was released from his three-year sentence.)

(on Albert Donoghue): 'The next time we saw him was at Bow Street Court as a prosecution witness giving evidence against us.'
(on himself): 'I was born to be violent.'

(on John McVicar): 'McVicar is a one-time small villain who makes his living writing and talking about real villains.'

(on Jack 'the Hat' McVitie): 'Only Ron and I know what happened to his body and we will take the secret to the grave with us. We will never incriminate other people; we will never grass on them the way people grassed on us to save their own skins. I didn't like the fellow. I wanted to get rid of him … He was very uncouth, he was loud and aggressive. There was just something I despised … A vexation to the spirit.'

(on Dennis Stafford): 'At the age of sixteen, both Ron and I were charged with assault [GBH] to Ronald Harvey and Dennis Seigenberg, both broke the code and made statements against us, although we were acquitted of the charge.'

RON KRAY

(on Broadmoor): 'Without my drugs, I go mad!'

(on the murder of George Cornell): 'I felt fucking marvellous. I have never felt so good, so bloody alive, before or since. Twenty years on and I can still recall every second of the killing of George Cornell.'

(on himself): 'Madness is a gift of life.'

(on the *Krays* film let-down): Ron lambasted the film after the subtitle 'If people are afraid of you, you can do anything' appeared on the video version of the big-screen film. Ron said: 'We used respect, not fear.'

THE KRAYS AND ME

(on Tony Lambrianou): 'He is nothing but a lackey and a grass. He grassed on us [the twins] when we were all locked up waiting for trial. He told Nipper Read that we did the murders and that it was nothing to do with him or his brother. He was never a member of the Firm, he never was a big gangster, he was nothing but an errand boy.'

(on Jack 'the Hat' McVitie): 'People like Tony Lambrianou may say they know how we got rid of him [i.e. McVitie's body]. But they don't. Only me and Reggie know, we won't tell, we never grass, we never have.'

(on Frank 'Mad Axeman' Mitchell): 'Freddie Foreman certainly did not pump Frank full of bullets and that was the conclusion of the court of law too. One day he will reappear and the world will know the truth.'

(on being implicated in the murder of the former light heavyweight champion of the world, Freddie Mills): 'He was shot in the right eye; the coroner's verdict was suicide. Freddie's wife believed the suicide to be a murder, but we never killed him or had anything to do with his death.'

(Michael Peterson – i.e. me!): 'When I was in Parkhurst with him, I saw him split open a screw's eye with one punch. Another time, he picked up a governor and ran away with him. The last I heard of him, some cons had done him over with a knife, but he refused to grass on them.'

(on Nipper Read's comment that Reg should not be released): 'He's just being spiteful. He's being a spiteful bastard. People like him want to see me and Reg down on our knees saying how sorry we are for all we've done … But we're not! They can stick their parole where it belongs!'

(on the Richardson gang): 'Some of the techniques used by the Richardson gang made the Kray twins look like Methodist lay preachers!'

(on Roy Shaw): 'He served three years in Broadmoor with me. While there, he broke a screw's jaw.'

BIBLIOGRAPHY

Cabell, Craig, *The Kray Brothers: The Image Shattered*.
London, Robson Books, 2002.

Campbell, John, *The Underworld*. London, BBC Books, 1994.

Dickson, John, *Murder without Conviction*. London, Sidgwick
& Jackson, 1986.

Dinenage, Fred, Kray, Ron and Reg, *Our Story*.
London, Sidgwick & Jackson, 1988.

Donoghue, Albert, and Short, Martin, *The Krays'
Lieutenant*. London, Pan Books, 1996.

Donoghue, Albert, and Short, Martin, *The Enforcer*.
London, Blake Publishing, 2002.

Fido, Martin, *Unfinished Business*. London, Carlton Books, 2001.

Fry, Colin, *The Kray Files*. London, Mainstream Publishing, 1998.

Fry, Colin, *The Krays: The Final Countdown*. London,
Mainstream Publishing, 2001.

Garner, Paul, *The Kray Twins Walk*. London, Louis London
Walks, 2002.

Glatt, John, *Evil Twins*. New York, St Martin's Press, 1999.

Hamilton, Lenny, *Branded by Ronnie Kray*. London, Blake
Publishing, 2002.

Hebdige, Dick, *The Kray Twins: A Study of Closure*. Birmingham, University Centre for Contemporary Cultural Studies, 1974.

Kelly, Patricia, and Morton, James, *The Barmaid's Tale*. London, Little, Brown & Co, 1996.

Kray, Charles, and McGibbon, Robin, *Me & My Brothers*. London, Grafton Books, 1988.

Kray, Charlie, and Fry, Colin, *Doing the Business*. London, Blake Publishing, 1999.

Kray, Kate, and Bruce, Mandy, *Murder, Madness and Marriage*. London, Blake Publishing, 1993.

Kray, Kate, *Lifers*. London, Blake Publishing, 1994.

Kray, Kate, *Married to the Krays*. Atlantic Transport Publishers, 1995.

Kray, Kate, *Free at Last*. London, Blake Publishing, 2000.

Kate, Kray, *The Twins: Men of Violence*. London, Blake Publishing, 2002.

Kray, Reggie, *Slang*. Wheel and Deal Publications, 1984.

Kray, Reggie, and Dinenage, Fred, *Our Story*. London, Pan Books, 1989.

Kray, Reggie, *Thoughts, Philosophy and Poetry*. London, River First, 1991.

Kray, Reggie, *Villains We Have Known*. London, Arrow, 1996.

Kray, Reggie, *A Way of Life*. London, Sidgwick & Jackson, 2000.

Kray, Roberta, *A Man Apart*. London, Sidgwick & Jackson, 2002.

Kray, Ronnie, and Dinenage, Fred, *My Story*. London, Sidgwick & Jackson, 1993.

Kray, Ronnie, *Sorted*. London, Blake Publishing, 1998.

Kray, Ronnie, *Born Fighter*. London, Century, 1990.

Lambrianou, Chris, and McGibbon, Robin, *Escape: from the Kray Madness*. London, Pan Books, 1996.

Lambrianou, Tony, and Clerk, Carol, *Inside the Firm*. London, Smith, Gryphon, 1992.

McConnell, Brian, *The Rise and Fall of the Brothers Kray*. Literary Services and Productions Ltd, 1969.

Morton, James, *Gangland*. London, Little, Brown & Co, 1992.